WHAT CHILDREN READ
IN SCHOOL

CRITICAL ANALYSIS
OF PRIMARY READING TEXTBOOKS

WHAT CHILDREN READ
IN SCHOOL

CRITICAL ANALYSIS
OF PRIMARY READING TEXTBOOKS

Edited by

Sara Goodman Zimet, Ed.D.

Reading Research Project Director
Assistant Professor of Psychiatry
University of Colorado
Medical Center
Denver, Colorado

Grune & Stratton
New York and London

Grune & Stratton, Inc.
111 Fifth Avenue
New York, New York 10003

Library of Congress Catalog Card Number 75-178589
International Standard Book Number 0-8089-0743-3

Printed in the United States of America

215197

CONTRIBUTORS

Gaston E. Blom, M. D.
Professor of Psychiatry and Education
Department of Psychiatry
University of Colorado Medical Center
Denver, Colorado

Cynthia Rose, M. D.
Clinical Instructor of Psychiatry
Department of Psychiatry
University of Colorado Medical Center
Denver, Colorado

Fred Busch, Ph. D.
Assistant Professor in Psychiatry
Department of Psychiatry
University of Michigan Medical Center
Children's Psychiatric Hospital
Ann Arbor, Michigan

v

Mrs. Stella Edge, M. A.
Librarian
Cherry Hills Elementary School
Denver, Colorado

Richard R. Waite, Ph. D.
Clinical Associate Professor of Psychology
Department of Psychiatry
University of Colorado Medical Center
Denver, Colorado

J. Lawrence Wiberg, M. D.
Clinical Instructor of Psychiatry
Department of Psychiatry
University of Colorado Medical Center
Denver, Colorado

Mrs. Marion Trost
Formerly, Research Assistant
Department of Psychiatry
University of Colorado Medical Center
Denver, Colorado

CONTENTS

FOREWORD

The appearance of this book raises a question: why have not systematic studies of the content of first grade readers appeared in the literature of curriculum research? After all, this book is not a consequence of recent theoretical or analytical breakthroughs. Furthermore, most of the questions raised in this book have been around for some decades.

The answer to the question has several components. The first is that systematic content analysis of educational materials has not been a favored research method in educational research. In light of the thousands of publications devoted to curriculum some readers may feel that what I have just said is quite unjustified. I would suggest to these readers that if they peruse the curriculum literature, they would find description rather than analysis, and those analyses they would find would tend to lack psychological sophistication and depth. Also, where one gets anything resembling content analysis it is usually in the context of some major event or process in the larger society, e.g., the first Russian Sputnik, or the emergence of poverty and race as national issues.

The second component of the answer is that the authors are *child* clinicians engaged in the most intimate ways with the thoughts, processes, and problems of children—and, as one would expect, many of the problems of the children involve learning in general and eductational tasks in particular. The kinds of content and clinical analyses contained in this book are, in a way, second nature to the authors as child clinicians. What a child is interested in, how he gets interested in it, the pervasive role of curiosity, the need for and problems of mastery, the conscious efforts of imitation and the preconscious processes of identification, and the ever-present problems of sexual identity and differentiation—these are just a sample of the problems, issues, and processes that make work with children a unique blend of fascination and frustration.

The second component takes on significance only in light of the third: the authors have for a number of years been totally engaged in running an educational setting for children. I refer specifically to the Day Care Center of the University of Colorado Medical Center, a psychoeducational facility for emotionally disturbed children of elementary school age, created by Dr. Blom. I have visited this setting a number of times and on each occasion marveled at the ability of the group to transcend the boundaries of their training and fields. They have not treated educational problems and processes as if they were secondary to intrapsychic phenomena—a rare feat indeed in a psychiatric setting.

The final component is as rare as the third: the willingness to subject hypotheses to systematic analyses. Only those who have never done research can view it as an exciting process and remain unaware that whatever excitement there is resides at the beginning point (formulating hypotheses) and at the end point (concluding that one has made a contribution to knowledge). Between these points are a lot of drudgery, false starts, and frustration. The conclusions presented in this book are important and exciting because they represent new knowledge with obvious consequences for education.

This book, however, is more than a contribution to education because the contribution it does make to education rests on the fact that a variety of methods (content analysis, formal observation, clinical analyses, cross-cultural comparisons) were used so as to achieve a rounded view of the problem. There are many studies which attack important problems with a single method, frequently with interesting results. But reliance on a particular method, however understandable that may be from a practical or financial standpoint, limits the scope of one's understanding of the problem and constricts the range of ideas which could guide further investigation. These authors have demonstrated well the fruitfulness of studying a problem with different methods. They have enriched our knowledge and understanding, and they have demonstrated how, through research, one can go about determining the content and the quality of the educational experience.

Seymour B. Sarason

Professor of Psychology
Yale University
New Haven, Connecticut

INTRODUCTION

Reading, the most researched subject in all educationdom, continues to stir a storm of controversy in a society that demands an increasingly literate populace. The relationship of literacy to a nation's economic and social development is generally recognized. Stimulated by the shockingly high estimates of reading retardation among elementary school students and high school dropouts, when, how, and what Johnny learns to read has become an issue of national concern and priority. This concern is summed up in the words of James Allen: "We should immediately set for ourselves the goal of assuring that by the end of the 1970's, the right to read shall be a reality for all—that no one shall be leaving our schools without the skill and the desire necessary to read to the full limits of his capability."

The search for the formula to teach the gifted and the slow, the retarded and the handicapped, the acculturated and the culturally distinct, continues despite the huge body of research accumulated thus far. Instead of seeking out one elegant solution, researchers have recognized the many intermingled factors involved in the reading process. Physiological factors, mental blocks, family reading habits, each has found a place in the literature. But the major thrust of the research has been in the area of teaching methodology. Despite the quantity of investigations carried out, the controversy over instructional procedures has continued to the point that it has been dubbed, at times, The Great Debate.

The research group whose work is represented in this book became interested in doing research in the area of reading as a result of their clinical work with children who had difficulties in reading. They were much impressed with the greater frequency of reading problems in boys than in girls, and with the difference being even higher in urban, nonwhite populations. Indeed, the sex ratios reported in the literature ranged from 3:1 to 10:1, boys always having a greater incidence of difficulty. These findings, however, did not hold in all countries or all cultures and this suggested that innate, sex-linked physiological variables were of limited, or at best indirect, importance. The findings focused the authors' attention on the materials used to teach first grade American school children to read.

Incredible as it may seem, the relationship of reading achievement to the substantive content of the reading textbook has received no systematic study whatsoever. A small body of experimental data has pointed to the impact of the content of reading texts on the child's lifespace. Not only is the content seen as a possible contributing factor in reading retardation, it is also seen as a transmitter of our cultural values and attitudes. In addition, a number of articles which appeared in the popular press have called attention to the many inappropriate elements in the content and format of reading textbooks. The main point of these writings is that the books used to reach reading to first graders are inappropriate culturally, developmentally, and socially. These criticisms, however, were based on impressions rather than on any extensive analysis of the material. Obviously the first job that needed to be done was to carefully describe the stories that make up beginning readers.

Aided initially by a grant from the National Institute for Mental Health, followed by grants from the Office of Education and the National Institute for Child Health and Human Development, this research group has, over the past six years, systematically investigated the substantive motivational and attitudinal content of first grade reading textbooks.

Much of the data collected from this research effort has been reported in various professional journals. However, these reports have reached only a limited, segmented audience. The purpose of this book is to present in a single source, an organized, integrated, and holistic portrait of the primary reading textbook as a learning motivator and transmitter of a culture's values and behavior standards. It was through the support of PHS Research Grant No. MH1674-01 from the Small Grants Section that the compilation of this book was made possible.

Chapter 1 describes the methods and the results of the analyses of 1,307 stories from twelve of the most widely used primary reading textbook series. It discusses the content in terms of hypotheses derived from initial clinical impressions. The first part describes the activities depicted—how appropriate they are for boys or for girls, how appropriate they are for children of the age of first graders, and how successfully the activities are carried out. Differences by publication date appeared, which influenced the findings in surprising ways. The second part completes the description of the texts and rounds out the Gestalt of the entire content of these first readers. The picture it presents shows a striking divergence from the realities of community, family, and child life and from what is known about child development.

The assumption underlying all of the research in this book is that reading textbooks whose content has little interest, appeal, or meaning for the child will impede his learning to read. In Chapter 2, the author presents a theoretical justification for this viewpoint and sets the pace for the two chapters that follow.

Once the motivational variables in the basal reading series were identified and described, it was of interest to determine how closely some of the characteristics coincided with the actual reading interests of children. Chapter 3 compares the content of the library book selections made by middle-class first grade students and the content of first grade reading textbooks.

Chapter 4 utilizes the information presented in Chapters 1, 2, and 3 to determine if first grade children do prefer the textbook stories which are developmentally appropriate. Five stories of high developmental relevance were paired with five stories of low developmental relevance along such content factors as theme, characters, sex, age, and outcome.

The pupils were asked to select the one in each pair they liked best. Their choices confirmed the hypothesis that developmentally appropriate stories are preferred.

During the past six years publishers have responded to the growing social pressures for reading textbooks that include as characters children of more than one ethnic background. The first such series is described in Chapter 5 along the dimensions discussed in Chapter 1 and then compared with the traditional all-white series.

While the original interest of the research group was on the influence of content on the development of reading skill, it also became apparent that cultural values and attitudes were being conveyed through the content as well. Thus Chapter 6 presents a detailed clinical analysis of some character types in the multiethinic series discussed in Chapter 5, and demonstrates that while the conscious intent of the authors was socially responsive, prejudicial values and attitudes clearly emerge in spite of their conscious efforts to avoid them.

Several more multiethnic texts appeared on the market since the series discussed in Chapters 5 and 6. The investigation expanded to include these new series, described in Chapter 7. They were subjected to the same analysis described in Chapters 1 and 4. Comparisons between series were made, and, where the same group of authors wrote both multiethnic series and traditional all-white series, comparisons were made between these series as well.

The thesis that reading texts are a means for acculturating the young and thereby require more thoughtfulness in the models of behavior they project is developed further in Chapter 8. The thesis is a result of the consistent findings related to ambiguity of sex role models in both the traditional and multiethnic series. The author was interested in finding out what models of sex role behavior were portrayed in the primary reading texts in wide use over a span of some 350 years. The coding dimensions used in the earlier studies required some modification and expansion in order to tap more adequately the sex role variables being investigated. Here, then, we have a useful perspective on a large sample of beginning reading texts used by many generations of American school children.

Chapter 9 presents the relationship between textbook content and the social values and attitudes held by the "establishment" from colonial days to the present. By examples drawn from the textbooks themselves, the author points out how the substantive content of the texts changed as America grew from a pioneer settlement to a highly industrialized, affluent nation.

The assumption that the content of primary reading textbooks communicates cultural, interpersonal, and individual attitudes and values, and that national differences do exist between primers from different countries led to the cross-national study reported in Chapter 10. Attitude profiles of thirteen countries are presented which give insight into national attitudes deemed worthy of inclusion in textbooks used to teach children how to read.

The implications of all the information culled from the various content analyses is the major focus in the final three chapters. In Chapter 11 the viewpoint is developed that elementary reading texts can perform a vital role in overcoming the discontinuities between childhood and adulthood, life in school and in the world outside school. Using "aggression" as an example of a developmental issue of concern to children, the author presents a carefully developed rationale, documented by history, the mass media, and the behavioral sciences, for the inclusion of aggression themes in elementary reading textbooks.

Chapter 12 discusses the issue of "meaningfulness" as it applies to the total educational experience as well as to textbook content. Correspondence between the author and textbook publishers is shared in an effort to point out the status of the "content of ideas" in these books and to suggest that "tradition" is the strongest determinant of what goes into the content and format of contemporary readers.

Within the framework of the manifold purposes for reading, Chapter 13 contains recommendations to textbook producers and consumers as to how they may improve textbook story content. Furthermore, as an additional source of guidance, two appendices follow this final chapter. Here the reader will find titles of tradebooks preferred by first graders from a middle-class, all-white suburban school and from an urban, all-black school.

The inescapable conclusion of all the chapters in this book is that we must begin to write textbooks that are effective as instruments both of acculturation and of teaching the reading skill.

S.G.Z.

We read to learn. We read to live another way.
We read to quench some blind and shocking fire.
We read to weigh the worth of what we have done
or dare to do. We read to share our awful
secrets with someone we know will not refuse
us. We read our way into the presence of great
wisdom, vast and safe suffering, or into the
untidy corners of another kind of life we fear
to lead.
—*Frank Jennings*

CHAPTER 1

WHAT THE STORY WORLD IS LIKE

Gaston E. Blom, Richard R. Waite,

Sara G. Zimet, and Stella Edge

Primers used in the schools have been the target of criticism, public scorn and ridicule, and journalistic jibes. The criticism is usually based on impressions. Some serious writers, however, have reflected at length on the weaknesses of primers—the dearth of content that is of moral value, the monotonous repetition of pleasant family activities, and the unrealistic portrayal of the social scene. Henry (1961) noted that primers conceal the realities of American culture and avoid critical problems of life. Bettelheim (1961) has written about other short-comings. He has complained that the stories have predictable outcomes, that they contradict the child's everyday experiences and offer no new knowledge, and thus do little to stimulate reading.

This Chapter combines two reports published originally as Blom, G. E., Waite, R. R., and Zimet, S. G., "Content of First Grade Reading Books," *The Reading Teacher*, 21: 317-23, 1968; and Waite, R. R., Blom, G. E., Zimet, S. G., and Edge, S., "First Grade Reading Textbooks," *Elementary School Journal*, 67: 366-74, 1967. Copyright © 1967 by the University of Chicago. Both reprinted by permission.

The study reported here is concerned with the value of the stories in developing children's interest in reading. It is assumed that the materials used to introduce children to reading influence their interest in reading. The importance of this influence probably varies from child to child. A child whose intellectual skills are adequate and who comes from a verbal family that values reading highly is likely to learn to read regardless of the teaching methods and materials he encounters, provided that he is comfortable with the values his family holds. Children who get little encouragement to read from their family and subculture frequently require continued help from the teacher to increase their desire to read. In this regard, the content of the stories that teachers first use is important in learning reading skills, but the content of stories is also important in maintaining interest in reading.

The research reported here is divided into two parts. The first is an examination of the activities depicted in the stories found in primary reading textbooks. The second focuses on the other story characteristics. The material analyzed is made up of the twelve most frequently used series of primers and preprimers (Hollins, 1955) which consisted of 1,307 stories in all. This group of stories made up more than 90 percent of the stories used in first grade classrooms in the United States (Hollins, 1955).

Manuals were devised for each dimension to be studied. In addition to the activity dimensions—age of child the activity depicted would appeal to, sex of child the activity would appeal to, and outcome of activity—three other dimensions were selected for study. These were the characters in the story, the theme or main activity, and the distribution of children in the stories according to sex, age, and family membership. Under "characters in the story," there are ten categories, among them Children Only, Animals Only, and Children and Mother. Under "theme or main activity," there are seventeen categories, among them Real Life Situations With Positive Affect, Pets, Aesthetic Activity, and Religious Activity.

The manual lists a large number of children's activities grouped according to: (1) the age at which children are most likely to engage in the activities and (2) the sex of children who prefer each activity. In constructing the manual, the four members of the research group pooled their judgments, which were based on their professional experiences as well as their observations as adults and as parents. Developmental data in the research literature were also used in constructing the manual. A behavioral item was included in the manual if all four researchers agreed on the age at which children are most likely to engage in it and on its appeal to boys or to girls.

The ratings of the outcome of the activity in each story are made as follows: If the main activity depicted in a story ends in the attainment of its goal, it is rated Success. If the goal is not achieved, it is rated Failure. If the goal is achieved only through the efforts of someone not initially involved in the activity (usually an older person), it is rated Help.

Two female graduate students, who were not told the purposes or the hypotheses of the study, coded the stories. In preparation for coding the stories, the raters were asked to use the manual to code a sample of stories and to discuss their judgments with a member of the research team. The raters then proceeded to code one series of books (134 stories) independently. Agreements between raters were computed. The results are presented in Table 1-1.

Table 1-1
Agreement Between Two Raters on 134 Stories

Coding Dimensions	Percent of Agreement
Character	99
Theme	86
Activity	
age	92
sex	94
outcome	94
Overall	93

Differences in judgments were discussed by the raters and one member of the research group. Special emphasis was given to "theme." Differences between the raters' understanding of several categories accounted for most of the disagreements in judging the themes of the stories. After the training, the raters divided the task of coding the remainder of the 1,307 stories.

A sizable number of the stories—599 out of 1,307—were originally coded Boy-Girl (appropriate for boys as well as girls). While this finding was of interest in itself, the raters were asked to try to judge each of these stories as appropriate for either boys or girls wherever possible.

Each rater did so for all stories; disagreements were resolved in conference.

I

The activities depicted in the stories found in primary reading textbooks were examined for: (1) how appropriate they are for boys or girls, (2) how appropriate they are for children the age of first graders, and (3) how successfully the activities are carried out. These three dimensions were chosen for several reasons. Among the most important considerations were research findings on the difference in the incidence of reading difficulty for boys and girls. In the United States, boys are much more likely to have problems in learning to read than are girls (Money, 1962). According to researchers, the number of boys who have trouble with reading is three times the number of girls who have trouble with reading. This phenomenon led the authors to an informal examination of primers to get an impression as to whether the stories would be less appealing to boys than to girls.

The examination led to several impressions. The first impression was that the descriptions of primers as pollyannaish, as representative of the upper-middle class, and as unrelated to real life situations have some truth. The second, that the stories depicted activities that in real life are most frequently engaged in by children younger than first graders. Rarely did the stories tell of activities appropriate for children older than first graders. The third, that the activities in the stories were usually activities in which girls rather than boys take part. The fourth, that stories in which children did not attain the constructive goals of the activities were common. The last impression was that the activities that boys most frequently engage in were the activities in which the goals were most frequently not achieved.

From these impressions three hypotheses were derived that could be tested by analyzing the content of a large number of stories. The following hypotheses, then, all concern the nature of the activities depicted in the stories:

1. The activities depicted in the stories are more frequently ones which are engaged in by children younger than six years of age than by children older than six in American society.
2. The activities are most frequently those in which girls engage.
3. The masculine activities depicted end in failure more frequently than the feminine activities do.

FINDINGS

Table 1-2 summarizes the distribution of judgments on the basis of appropriateness for children of the age of first graders. To test the first hypothesis, it was necessary to assign half of the six-to-seven year ratings to each year in order to arrive at a frequency which would reflect correctly the number of stories in which the main activity was appropriate for children older than six years. Thus, the frequency for age six is 273.5, and for age seven is 273.5. The results show no appreciable difference between the number of stories in which the activities were judged as appropriate for children older than six years and the number of stories rated as appropriate for children younger than six years of age. The first hypothesis, therefore, is not supported by the data. The stories do not predominantly depict activities appropriate for preschoolers.

Table 1-2

Appropriateness of Main Activity, Classified by Age

Age Group:	2-3	4-5	6-7	8-9	10-11	Total
Number of Stories	23	497	547	226	14	1,307

Table 1-3 summarizes the distribution of the original judgments and the forced judgments of the appropriateness of the stories for boys or girls. The results offer no support for the second hypothesis, that more stories are appropriate for girls than for boys. The large number of stories falling into the Boy-Girl category (46 percent of the total) on the original ratings do suggest, however, that the stories do not emphasize the differences in the roles of boys and girls.

Table 1-3

Appropriateness of Main Activity, Classified by Sex

Group:	Boy	Girl	Boy-Girl	Total
Number of Stories	339	369	599	1,307

The results presented in Table 1-4 show a statistically significant interaction between the appropriateness of a story for boys or girls and the success or failure of the activity depicted (χ^2 = 23.8, p<.001).

Inspection of this table indicates that the overall interaction is most strongly influenced by the relationship between the appropriateness of the activities depicted for boys or girls on the one hand and the success or failure of the activities on the other. The procedure described by Castellan (1965) for the partitioning of contingency tables was used to determine whether this specific interaction was significant ($\chi^2 = 8.76$, $p<.005$) and to account for most of the overall interaction. This finding supports the third hypothesis, that is, activities appropriate for boys end in failure more frequently than do activities appropriate for girls.

Table 1-4

Appropriateness of Main Activity, Classifed by Outcome

	Outcome				Total Number of Stories
	Success	*Failure*	*Help*	*Unclassified*	
Boy	379	181	56	4	620
Girl	394	135	54	2	585
Boy-Girl	64	30	4	4	102
Total	837	346	114	10	1,307

To understand why the first two hypotheses failed to gain support, the authors reexamined the data. Both hypotheses (the hypothesis on the appropriateness of an activity for six-year-olds and the hypothesis on the appropriateness of an activity for boys or girls) were derived from a review and preliminary investigation of the primers in only two series. In the reexamination by the authors every series was studied. The two series from which the hypotheses were derived were published in the 1950's. A number of series used in the present study were published more recently. Since the newer series may have differed from the series published earlier, the series published in 1961 or before were compared with the series published after 1961.

Table 1-5 shows the frequency with which stories, grouped by date of publication, were rated as appropriate for children younger than six, for six-year-olds, and for children older than six years of age.

Table 1-5

**Appropriateness of Main Activity, Classified by
Age Group and Publication Date**

Publication Date	Age Group			Total Number of Stories
	Under Six	*Six Years*	*Over Six*	
1956-1961	313	140	238	691
1962-1963	207	133.5	275.5	616
Total	520	273.5	513.5	1,307

The interaction between publication date and the age of children for whom the activity is appropriate is significant ($\chi^2 = 20.2$, p<.005). Clearly, the data obtained from primers published before 1961 support the hypothesis that stories tend to depict activities appropriate for children younger than six years of age. The results obtained from the series published after 1961 indicate a noteworthy shift toward activities appropriate for older children. The writers of children's primers may have changed the nature of their content sometime around 1961.

Table 1-6 shows the relationship between publication date and sex of child for whom the main activity was rated as appropriate. (The ratings on appropriateness of main activity for boys and girls included forced ratings.) Here again, the interaction is significant ($\chi^2 = 17.4$, p<.001). The second hypothesis is supported by the data for the series published before 1961; the data for primers published after 1961 do not support the second hypothesis. The activities depicted in the series published before 1961 were most frequently activities in which, in American culture, girls engage. The activities in the series published after 1961 were not most frequently activities in which, in American culture, girls engage.

Tables 1-7 and 1-8 show the publication date of the series, appropriateness of activities for boys or girls, and success or failure of the activities. The overall interaction between appropriateness of activities for boys and girls and success or failure of the activities is

Table 1-6

**Appropriateness of Main Activity, Classified by
Sex and Publication Date**

Publication Date	Boy	Girl	Boy-Girl	Total Number of Stories
1956-1961	280	350	61	691
1962-1963	340	235	41	616
Total	620	585	102	1,307

significant in the series published before 1961 (χ^2 = 20.6, p<.005). When Table 1-7 is partitioned, the chief source of this significant interaction (χ^2 = 9.42, p<.005) is found to be the interaction between the appropriateness of activities for boys or girls on the one hand, and success or failure of the activities on the other. In Table 1-8, the overall interaction between sex and outcome is not statistically significant in the series published after 1961 (χ^2 = 11.0, p>.05). When Tables 1-7 and 1-8 are compared, the third hypothesis is supported by the series published before 1961, the activities appropriate for boys ended in failure more frequently than the activities appropriate for girls. For the series published after 1961, the activities appropriate for boys did not end in failure more frequently than the activities appropriate for girls.

Table 1-7

**Appropriateness of Main Activity, Classified by
Sex and Outcome for 1956-1961**

Appropriateness	Outcome				Total Number of Stories
	Success	Failure	Help	Undecided	
Boy	182	77	18	3	280
Girl	262	61	26	1	350
Boy-Girl	42	12	4	3	61
Total	486	150	48	7	691

Table 1-8

**Appropriateness of Main Activity, Classified by
Sex and Outcome for 1962-1963**

	Outcome				Total Number of Stories
Appropriateness	*Success*	*Failure*	*Help*	*Undecided*	*Stories*
Boy	197	104	38	1	340
Girl	132	74	28	1	235
Boy-Girl	22	18	0	1	41
Total	351	196	66	3	616

The results indicate that hypotheses on appropriateness of activities for six-year-olds and for boys or girls are supported in the primers published before 1961. That is, in the six series of primers published between 1956 and 1961, the stories depict activities that are characteristic of girls of preschool age more often than not. Furthermore, activities preferred by boys end in failure more frequently than do activities preferred by girls.

DISCUSSION

The relationship between these findings and the value of the stories in stimulating an interest in reading remains a question for empirical research. One could speculate, however, that the six-year-old entering the new world of school—which emphasizes growing up, new accomplishments, knowledge, and skills, and which slights dependency gratification and preschool interests—would find these stories in conflict with his new-found values. Moreover, developmental research indicates that by the sixth year, most children are following interests generally preferred by their sex. Certain interests, fantasies, and personality reactions typical of either boys or girls are well documented and generally accepted (Kagan, 1964). These differences are thought to result in part from innate factors but to a larger extent from cultural expectations and reinforcements. Boys have identified with, or are identifying with, their fathers, and girls, with their mothers. Boys are caught up in the pursuit of masculine activities; their play reflects masculine interests; they choose male peers for friends, and they avoid close relationships with girls. Primers that depict more feminine than masculine activities could hardly be attractive to boys.

Another finding that applies to all the series examined in this study is directly related to the picture of the six-year-old child presented here. As Table 1-3 shows, in the original judgments of the appropriateness of an activity for boys or girls, 46 percent, or 599, of the stories were judged as depicting activities that boys as well as girls customarily engage in. One would speculate that the lack of differentiation in sex roles indicated by this finding conflicts with one of the primary developmental tasks that confront the first grader, that of specifying, maintaining, and reinforcing his own appropriate sex role. One could argue that a story is useful in inspiring the child to want to read in proportion to the clarity of the presentation of sex role. The primers studied here may have little value in encouraging a child to learn to read, partly because the books attempt to present stories for girls as well as boys.

From a psychoanalytic viewpoint the adoption of a stable sex role indicates the resolution of oedipal conflict and the availability of drives for other types of learning. Anastasiow (1965) demonstrated in a sample of children from lower- and upper-middle-class homes that boys with strong masculine values and interests as measured by picture preference, boy preference, and Franky Fable tests have significantly higher reading scores in first grade than boys with median and feminine role scores. This finding suggests that the content of first grade stories should emphasize activities that are clearly either masculine or feminine.

The findings related to year of publication came as something of a surprise. Do they reflect a change in the content of stories selected for primers? The question can be answered only by further studies. Content analyses might be made of two editions of a series, one edition published before 1961 and a revised edition published after 1961. Support for the idea that the content of primers changed about 1961 would be consistent with the reorientation of education in the late 1950's, which took cognizance of the frequency of reading disabilities in boys, the growing public criticism of reading textbooks in scholarly articles and in the popular press and television, and the research on differences in the learning patterns of boys and girls.

Although the study reported here does not include analyses of various revisions of a series, it does include two series published by the same company, one in 1956 and one in 1962. According to the Hollins study (1955), the earlier series was by far the most frequently used in school systems throughout the United States in the 1950's. Discussions with teachers and the number of book orders placed by one large urban school system in 1964 suggest that this company continues as the largest supplier of first grade primers. A comparison of the two editions supports the idea that between 1956 and 1962 the content of the stories was changed. In the earlier edition more of the activities in the stories were rated younger and feminine. In both editions, however, masculine stories ended in failure more frequently than feminine stories did. This particular publisher, at least, currently puts greater emphasis on masculine content, though he continues to depict the frustration of masculine accomplishment.

II

The dimensions investigated in this part of the study included reading level, story themes, environmental setting of the story, several attributes of characters in the stories, sex of the activity depicted in the stories, age of these activities, outcome of these activities, agent of failure or frustration, and object of failure or frustration.

FINDINGS

Theme

Table 1-9 lists the 17 theme categories in order by frequency of ratings. The stereotyped quality of these stories and books is indicated by the large proportion of stories contained in the first three categories (47 percent). In nine of the twelve series, these three categories accounted for over 40 percent of the stories. The category, Real Life with Positive Emotions, may also be described as "Pollyanna" stories. It was ranked first in eight series. Quiet Activities, Pranks and Humor, School, Parties, Lessons from Life, and Aesthetic Appreciation were all in low frequency. School accounted for 3 percent of the stories with five series having no stories about school. There were no stories about religion. There was only one story out of 1,307 that depicted a religious setting or characters (sitting in church), but the major theme concerned a pet. A finding such as this might be explained by society's insistance on the separation of religion and education. This is in contrast to the content of primers used in colonial America where religious content dominated (see Chap. 9). Furthermore, the theme category, Lessons from Life, did not appear in seven of the twelve first grade reading series and is in striking low frequency in the remaining five. It would appear that moral and ethical values are not dealt with directly through the themes of stories. Again this is in contrast to readers used in the past. While there were some folk-tale themes in the stories, they consisted of animals with human characteristics and other anthropomorphized figures such as toys, flowers, trains, buses, and pancakes. In summary, one might conclude that neutral "Pollyanna" stories predominate and that there is a striking absence of stories which directly convey moral, ethical, and cultural values.

Table 1-9
Frequency Ratings—Themes

Themes	Stories	Percentage	Themes	Stories	Percentage
Real Life with					
Positive Emotions	303	23	Work Projects	76	6
Active Play	162	12	Quiet Activities	41	3
Pets	152	12	Pranks & Humor	37	3
Outings	107	8	School	35	3
Imaginative Play	95	7	Parties	20	2
Real Life with					
Negative Emotions	93	7	Aesthetics	7	.5
Nature	83	6	Unclassified	3	.5
Folk Tales	78	6	Religion	0	0

When the theme data were examined in relation to the dimensions of sex of the activity and outcome of the activity, other findings appear. Sex of the activity is a classification of a story based on a stereotypical notion of what boys would do or be interested in (Boy), what girls would do or be interested in (Girl), or what both boys and girls would do or be interested in (Boy-Girl). When stories were rated Boy-Girl, these stories were recoded in an attempt to reassign them to either Boy or Girl wherever possible (that is, a forced sex rating was made).

A large number of stories were in the Boy-Girl category (46 percent) as compared to Boy category (26 percent), and Girl category (28 percent), which suggests an ambiguity in sex role in relation to the activities depicted. When a forced sex rating was made, the distribution of 48 percent Boy, 45 percent Girl, and 7 percent Boy-Girl was obtained. It is referred to as Expected Sex Distribution. Eight theme categories show striking deviations from this distribution. Active Play, Outings, Pranks, and Work Projects were related to the Boy category. Quiet Activities, School, Folk Tales, and Real Life with Positive Emotions were related to the Girl category. These relationships show some sex role appropriateness in relation to activities. The School theme shows twice as many Girl stories (63 percent) as Boy stories (31 percent). In the early period of American history, literacy and formal education had been associated with masculine prerogatives; the association of school with girlish activities appears to be the contemporary one. This is an inappropriate value to stress if there is real concern with promoting positive relationships between school and boy-associated activities.

Outcome of an activity is the classification of a story based on whether the activity or purpose is accomplished (Success) or not (Failure). A third category, Help, includes those situations where the activity or purpose is about to be frustrated but is finally accomplished.

The outcome of the activity for all 1,307 stories has a distribution of 64 percent Success, 26 percent Failure, and 9 percent Help. It was referred to as Expected Outcome Distribution. Ten theme categories had deviations from this distribution. As expected, Real Life with Positive Emotions had a high success outcome (77 percent), and Real Life with Negative Emotions a low success outcome (39 percent). High success was associated with Outings, Pranks, Quiet Activities, and School. Low success was related to Pets, Active Play, Imaginary Play, and Work Projects.

If one considers outcome as a type of reinforcement (i.e., Success is positive and Failure is negative), it is of interest that Quiet Play was positively reinforced while Active Play and Imaginative Play were not. In examining the Work Project stories (N=76), those associated with failure outcomes (N=33) had two and one-half times as many Boy stories as Girl stories. In these failure stories, animals were the agents of failure in sixteen instances.

Characters

In the character dimension there are ten categories as shown in Table 1-10. Again, the categories are presented in order of frequency. The first three categories constitute 53 percent of the stories. In eight of the twelve series these three categories accounted for over 50 percent of the stories, indicating a restriction in range of character combinations. Children and Animal stories were found 20 percent or more in eight series. In strikingly low frequency were stories with Make-Believe Characters (six of twelve series had no such stories), with Inanimate Objects (six had no stories), and with Adults Only (four had no stories). There were nearly twice as many stories in the Children and Mother category (16 percent) as Children and Father (9 percent).

Table 1-10
Frequency Ratings—Characters

Characters	Stories	Percentage
Children and Animals	296	23
Children and Mother	202	16
Children, Mother, and Father	188	14
Children and Other Adults	172	13
Children Only	146	11
Children and Father	112	9
Adults Only	27	2
Make-Believe Characters	14	1
Inanimate Objects	11	1

When the data on characters were examined in relation to other dimensions, Animals Only stories correlated very highly with four- and five-year-old activities (81 percent). Furthermore, Children and Animal stories had a low percentage of success outcome (52 percent). These are usually stories where pets frequently frustrate the intentions and wishes of children although the frustration is typically reacted to with amusement.

Distribution of Children

The ratings on the Distributions of Children dimension are summarized in Table 1-11. Of the 1,307 stories, 1,161 involved children as characters, solely or in combination with others. Using pictures and story content these 1,161 stories were rated according to sex (boy or girl), age (6 years, < 6 years, > 6 years), and family membership of the children (family and nonfamily). There were twelve categories and the number of children in each category for every story was recorded. The final data, however, were reported as the number of stories in which the category is represented.

Table 1-11
**Distribution of Children According to Sex,
Age, and Family Membership**

Categories	*Stories*	*Percentage (of a total of 1161)*
Boy: 6, Family	897	77
Girl: 6, Family	837	72
Girl: <6, Family	389	34
Boy: 6, Nonfamily	340	29
Girl: 6, Nonfamily	278	25
Boy: <6, Family	69	6
Boy: <6, Nonfamily	64	5.5
Boy: >6, Nonfamily	38	3
Girl: <6, Nonfamily	29	2.5
Girl: >6, Nonfamily	9	.8
Boy: >6, Family	9	.8
Girl: >6, Family	4	.3

"Little sister," (Girl: <6, Family), appeared in 34 percent of stories while "little brother," (Boy: <6, Family), appeared in 6 percent. "Big brother," (Boy: >6, Family), occurred in .8 percent of stories whereas "big sister," (Girl: >6, Family), in .3 percent. The stories typically had boy and girl characters at six years of age. When other child characters appeared there was a great prevalence of younger children and a relative absence of older children. In strikingly high frequency were girls less than age six. If we consider the child reader as identifying with the characters in the stories, then these distributions would tend to support either age-appropriate or younger identifications. In strikingly low frequency were stories where only one child was present, indicating that a child almost always appears with other children.

The stories were rated according to whether the characters in an individual story were Family Only, Nonfamily Only, and Family and Nonfamily. The results indicated that 692 were Family Only, 65 Nonfamily Only, and 410 Family and Nonfamily. Another method of determining family and nonfamily characteristics was to total the stories in Child Family and Child Nonfamily categories. Child Family stories totaled 2,205 while Child Nonfamily stories were 758. These results together demonstrate the family centeredness of the characters.

Environmental Setting

The stories were rated according to the environmental setting in which they occurred. There are five categories in this dimension: Urban, Suburban, Rural, Not Clear as to setting, and Other. Suburban accounted for 38 percent of the stories while Urban was in extremely low frequency (1 percent). Rural accounted for 20 percent of the stories. These distributions can be compared to those of the actual population in the United States: Suburban, 33 percent; Rural, 36 percent; and Urban, 31 percent (Metropolitan Life, 1966).

The Not Clear category (35 percent) consisted of stories where the setting was indoors, where the setting constantly shifted (i.e., travelling by car, bus, or train, or where the setting could be a playground). The category Other (6 percent), included make-believe (N=66), foreign country (N=6), on train or ship (N=4), and seashore (N=1).

Reading Level

The content analyses show no differences across reading levels—preprimer, primer, first reader. In fact, 61 percent of the stories are in books classified as Primer 1 and First Reader. Therefore, it is these stories which influence the overall findings. The authors believe that content should not be influenced by reading level. One can present realistic, age-appropriate, and high motivational interesting reading materials at early levels.

DISCUSSION

It is possible to describe a Gestalt for the stories in this original national sample of commonly used first grade readers in the United States. The activities are neutral and redundant without much content significance and variation. They are happy-family centered and tend to be ambiguous as to sex role. A child is most always with other children and is seldom alone. Older children as siblings and peers rarely appear. In contrast, there tends to be a regressive pull through the emphasis on family attachment and younger siblings, animal stories, anthropomorphized figures, and ambiguity in sex role. The setting is most typically in the suburbs, rarely in the city, and usually in and around a home. Pets are amusing, cute, and frustrating nuisances.

This Gestalt represents a striking divergence from the realities of community, family, and child life and from what is known about child development. Most children live in cities and are in contact with other children of different racial and national backgrounds. Family life is not so exclusively child centered, nor is it constantly happy and smiling. Parents punish and children display a range of emotions. It is most unusual to find fraternal twins in the same family (i.e., boy and girl of age six) and it is more typical to find older siblings and peers in greater frequency than the first grade readers demonstrate. Pets have various meanings to children—they can be companions in adventure, exploration, and rough play, and they can be the means of learning about biology (pregnancy, birth, infancy, growth, weaning, toilet training, old age, death, illness, and injury). The stories obviously do not deal with these issues.

The child early in the latency period of his development (ages six and seven) shows many behaviors reflecting considerable independence and strong sex role appropriateness. Boys in particular avoid girls and girls' activities, while girls may be more tomboyish and more willing to associate with boys. The latency age child spends increasingly more time away from home and is less family centered. He is curious and interested in the world around him, both human and nonhuman. He seeks information about that world. Heroism, adventure, and make-believe other than anthropomorphized animals also interest him.

Unlike the activity dimension discussed in the first part of this chapter, the content analyses of theme, characters, environmental setting, and their interactions with other dimensions show no particular change between books published before or after 1961. It would appear that writers of textbooks for children need to show greater sophistication and awareness of the developmental interests of children and the real life of children and their families.

REFERENCES

Anastasiow, N. J. "Success in school and boys' sex-role patterns." *Child Development*, 1965, *36*, 1053-1066.

Bettelheim, B. "The decision to fail." *School Review*, 1961, *69*, 377-412.

Castellan, N. J. "On the partitioning of contingency tables." *Psychological Bulletin*, 1965, *64*, 330-338.

Henry, J. "Reading for what?" Claremont Reading Conference, *Twenty-Fifth Yearbook*. Claremont, Cal.: Claremont Graduate School Curriculum Laboratory, 1961, pp. 19-38.

Hollins, W. H. "A national survey of commonly used first-grade readers." Unpublished data, Alabama A & M College, 1955.

Kagan, J. "Acquisition and significance of sex typing and sex role identity." In M. L. Hoffman & L. W. Hoffman (eds.), *Review of child development research*. New York: Russell Sage Foundation, 1964, pp. 137-167.

Metropolitan Life Insurance Company, personal communication, 1966.

Money, J. (ed.). *Reading disability: progress and research needs in dyslexia*. Baltimore: Johns Hopkins Press, 1962.

CHAPTER 2

INTEREST, RELEVANCE, AND LEARNING TO READ

Fred Busch

The question must be asked why interest and relevance should play a role in learning to read. Various educators such as McCracken and Walcutt (1963), in their definition of reading do not seem to consider the content of what is being read of particular importance in the child's learning to read. It is the thesis of this chapter that content is of crucial significance in the process of learning to read, and that interest and relevance are significant content variables. Even McCracken and Walcutt while emphasizing the importance of the instructional process in learning to read, imply that there is a need for the young learner to read stories that include rewarding content. In an attempt to specify the importance of interest and relevance in learning to read, each will be treated separately for the purpose of clarity. However, these must be considered interdependent issues.

This chapter first appeared, in its original version, as: Busch, F. "Basals Are Not for Reading," *Teachers College Record*, 72: 23-30, 1970. Reprinted by permission.

INTEREST

It would seem self-evident that story content of interest to a child (i.e., content of importance that excites curiosity and attention) would facilitate the process of learning to read. The one study made in this area is encouraging but not conclusive (Whipple, 1963). Although in the Whipple study a new multiethnic reader compared favorably to a traditional primer on various tests of reading skill and interest appeal, the small actual differences and lack of follow-up to determine long-range effects make the data inconclusive.

In order to look at the role of interest in learning to read one must first look at the motivations of a child in learning to read. Namnum and Prelinger (1961) point out that discussions of motives for learning to read are conspicuously absent in most writings dealing with the teaching of reading. For the most part, the concept that a child will be motivated to learn to read is usually taken for granted. In their review of the literature on why children learn to read, the authors do mention, however, two motives implicitly discussed by various writers. The first of these can be broadly defined as the child's relationship to adults. That is, due to the social pressure adults put on the child to learn to read, and the child's need to win approval from adults and to strongly identify with adult activities, the child will want to learn to read. The second motivational factor has to do with the child's need for mastering his surroundings. In other words, the child faced with a new situation like reading will, because of his particular developmental stage, want to master the task. While not disagreeing with these motivations as important factors in learning to read, there are dangers in depending upon these as the child's only motives when teaching him to learn to read.

If the child's motives for reading are viewed only as a reaction to external pressures or psychic needs, while the motivational qualities inherent in the reading process are ignored, then the *process* of learning to read can become an end in itself. The complex task of translating perception of symbols into vocalizations and thoughts is something that can totally involve the child. Thus, if "learning to read" is presented to the child as an autonomous process that is unrelated to anything in particular, once this challenge is past, the child will lose interest. That is, if by "learning to read" one has met the expectations of society and satisfied the need for mastery, then reading can become unimportant or irrelevant.

What if one tried to stimulate and then capitalize on the child's interest in the content of what is to be read, and this was made an inherent part of learning to read? The purpose of learning to read then would not only be "learning to read," but also would be to direct the child's curiosity and attention to the whole range of experiences available through reading, including obtaining information. That this is where the child starts his involvement with reading can be seen by observing a toddler's introduction to books. His involvement is not with how the material is communicated from the printed word, but with the interest the content provides for him. By teaching the child with material of little interest or with an emphasis on mechanics, we would seem to be clearly delineating between work and play, school and nonschool experiences. This is of questionable worth both education-ally and psychologically. More than fifty years ago, Dewey (1916) warned against the danger of isolating the child's experiences in school from those outside the school, especially in the early years. In similar terms to the discussion above, he cautioned against the problems inherent in material unrelated to immediate and direct experience, and warned against media of representation becoming ends in themselves. From a psychological point of view, to arbitrarily separate work from play (in its broadest sense), is not to use the child's developmental involvement with each (Freud, 1965). Furthermore, for the child only recently able to put off need gratification for any length of time, and just discovering means of receiving gratifications in modified fashion (Panel Report, 1957), the demand to put off pleasure in the task of reading for some unspecified future gain is, at best, inconsistent with the child's developmental readiness to meet a demand.

In a recent study of children who are successful readers (McCarthy et al., 1963) the authors point out that these children most often come from homes where reading is an important aspect of the parents' life, and where the children are included in numerous experiences involving books (i.e., they are frequently read to, books are given as gifts on special occasions, the library habit is established early, etc.). While most educators have probably suspected this for a long time, its full implications seem never to have been realized or capitalized upon. It would seem that the most heuristic interpretation of the McCarthy et al. data would be that these children have already been shown the purposes behind learning to read, both through adult example and their own experience. If a child has already been shown that books can be interesting and of value to him, then important motivational factors for learning to read exist from the beginning. It then becomes the school's task to stimulate the child who has not come from the type of background identified above by interesting him in the content as well as the process of reading, and thus specifying the purposes. Again, if the child can see the value to him of the content of the books, the process of learning to read is then more meaningful.

It does not seem to be a very bold prediction to state that other media beside the printed word have and will increasingly take over the role of disseminators of information and conveyors of intellectual enjoyment and emotional experience. As this occurs, it will become clear to schools that they must interest the child not only in the process of reading but in its purposes as well, or reading will become the Edsel of the school system. In looking at McLuhan's discussions of television (1967), one can see that television's attraction to children, when compared to first grade reading texts, is that its purposes are inherent in the process itself. The boundary between the *how* and *why* of television simply does not exist. *How* to learn to read is taught, but *why* seems left to the child's previous experiences—experiences that may be slowly disappearing.

RELEVANCE

That the content of first grade reading texts is bland and pollyannaish (see Chap. 1) implies that their authors believe that the child learning to read is like a precariously balanced object that will tip if touched even lightly. That is, they believe that the child will be harmed in some way if books confront him with the issues he is experiencing and living in his daily life. That nothing is further from the truth can be documented by the writings on the needs and developmental tasks of latency age children.

Erikson (1959) discusses the importance in this stage of the need for mastery and how the child's personality crystalizes around the idea, "I am what I learn." What the child needs to master and has to learn during this stage is not only the rational, practical techniques and means of behavior that allow for a feeling of being part of the adult world, but also a means of dealing with one's inner world. For example,

Erikson, in discussing play, talks of the importance of a child mastering objects in the toy world and how this becomes associated with the mastery of conflicts, resulting in an experiential feeling of prestige for the child. This allows the child to advance to new stages of mastery not restricted to toys and objects, but which "includes an infantile way of mastering experiences by meditating, experimenting, planning, and sharing." What Erikson is saying, then, is that the child needs to have the feeling of mastery of conflict at this stage of development. Most important is that the child's normal developmental concerns during this period lead him to be both interested and involved in mastering his inner as well as his outer world. The results of each are inextricably intertwined.

Other psychoanalytic writers (Blos, 1962; Buxbaum, 1951; Friedenberg, 1957), while not discussing latency in the descriptively illuminating language that Erikson uses, view the crucial aspects of the latency age period in an essentially similar way. For them the most important issue for the latency age child is the development of mechanisms which allow for adaptive behavior that is increasingly oriented toward reality. The child is driven to find means of dealing with the conflicts of the present and earlier stages of development in order that growth may occur. Although external factors certainly exist, this process is primarily viewed as determined by internal factors that drive the child toward a mastery that will allow both for the unfolding of the socialization process and for the child to become progressively less dependent upon the external world for controls. The key for these writers, as with Erikson, is the development of healthy mechanisms (i.e., ego functions) for the child's ability to cope with what is going on inside of him and with the realities of the external world, as well as the interaction of these two.

From what is known about the child's learning to read, it would seem that the content of first grade reading texts should include the developmental concerns of children and the mastery of issues that are crucial to them. That this type of content is not something that will frighten the child, but to the contrary, will intrigue him, is not just a hypothesis based upon knowledge of latency, but is supported by others. Although Zimet (1966) has pointed to the difficulties in research on children's reading preferences, two studies seem relevant here, Friedlander (1942) and Peller (1958). These authors, in discussing children's stories which have successfully endured over time, mention two important factors in them: the stories are related to the developmental concerns of latency age children (Friedlander, 1942) and at the core of each story there is a universal daydream containing within it the conflicts with which each child must struggle (Peller, 1958). It would seem, indeed, that the child is drawn to stories that include the conflicts of the type he is experiencing and which current first grade reading texts strenuously avoid. While Friedlander and Peller stress the importance of instinctual gratification in the stories they identify as enduring, this seems to be only a partial answer. Although it is true that areas of conflict contain elements of gratification, the essential nature of conflict is that it is painful. A more complete conceptualization of the child's interest in stories with conflictual themes can be viewed in Eriksonian terms. As in the child's play where he projects conflicts on toys and uses these in the mastery process, the child can use the story characters in conflict to identify with, utilizing the pain itself as well as the solution to aid in mastery.

Peller has pointed out how stories which have been read and enjoyed by successive generations of latency age boys repeat, on a larger scale, everyday experiences that are difficult to cope with. One recurrent theme in these stories is that of the latency age boy, apart from his parents, who encounters adult figures representing the whole spectrum of character types in situations of varying degrees of danger. This theme depicts, in an exaggerated fashion, the quality of experiences that are common to most latency age boys. First of all the latency age boy is starting, on a consistent basis, to leave the protective influence of home for increasingly extended periods of independence. Secondly, he is coming in contact with numerous types of authority figures in school, community, and church. Thirdly, if nothing else, the uniqueness of the many new situations that the latency age boy must face causes much anxiety and perceived danger. In the exaggerated situations, the story's hero is usually portrayed as clever, resourceful, and virtuous, with his actions resulting in triumph. One can see, then, how the story communicates to the latency age boy that he does have some control over and power in his environment and that he has qualities that are uniquely his own which allows him to successfully adapt. In summary, a simple theme related to developmental concerns of latency age boys can be extremely beneficial. There is the sharing of a series of anxiety-provoking, painful experiences common, in a qualitative fashion, to most latency age boys. This in itself can prove to be helpful. Most important, there is the main character's ability to cope with difficult experiences. The latency age boy can thus gain the impetus for dealing more actively with his own conflicts, both through identification and example. The problems he is facing no longer have to seem so ominous or insurmountable. Although solutions aren't offered, the process of resolving conflict is presented as a possibility that should intrigue the child desirous of mastery.

What are the dangers when first grade reading texts avoid areas that are germane to the developmental concerns of children learning to read? Pearson (1952), using a psychoanalytic model to discuss learning problems, points to the difficulties that arise when an external situation does not hold the attention of a child. He states, "an important function of the ego is to direct attention to a particular situation or stimulus in order to master it (p. 334)." When the child is faced with a stimulus that he can respond to, the multitude of other stimuli which exist at the same time, but which do not have potential responses can be deflected. However, if no such situation or stimulus of importance is present, the child appears distracted and uninterested. First grade reading texts, by not addressing themselves to the content appropriate to the ego functioning of the latency age child and the need to get on with the process of mastery of the external and internal world, further complicates "learning to read."

Probably the most important weakness in the current content of most first grade reading texts revolves around the whole growth and maturation process. Various authors (Blos, 1962; Erikson, 1959; Havighurst, 1952) have pointed out that certain tasks in latency are important for further development in adolescence and adulthood. Books could certainly be helpful to the first grade child in dealing with the conflicts he is primed to master during this stage. This hypothesis has been supported in general terms by numerous investigators (Bender & Lourie, 1941; Cianciolo, 1956; Martin, 1955; Mattera, 1961; Witty, 1964). However, the bland, pollyannaish content found in most first grade reading texts not only stifles the growth process, but more importantly may communicate to the child that this must be something to be frightened of and avoided. Why else would the characters not show emotion that is negative as well as positive, feel anxiety and pain, or experience conflicts?

REFERENCES

Bender, L., & Lourie, R. "The effect of comic books on the idealogy of children." *American Journal of Orthopsychiatry*, 1941, *11*, 540-550.

Blos, P. *On adolescence.* New York: Free Press of Glencoe, 1962.

Buxbaum, E. "A contribution to the psychoanalytic knowledge of the latency period." *American Journal of Orthopsychiatry*, 1951, *21*, 182-198.

Cianciolo, P. J. "Children's literature can affect coping behavior." *Personnel and Guidance Journal*, 1956, *43*, 897-903.

Dewey, J. *Democracy and education.* New York: Macmillan, 1916.

Erikson, E. H. "Identity and the life cycle." *Psychological Issues*, 1959, *1*, 82-88.

Freud, A. *Normality and pathology in childhood.* New York: International Universities Press, 1965.

Friedenberg, F. S. "Thoughts on the latency period." *Psychoanalytic Review*, 1957, *44*, 390-400.

Friedlander, K. "Children's books and their function in latency and prepuberty." *American Imago*, 1942, *3*, 129-150.

Havighurst, R. J. *Developmental tasks and education.* New York: McKay, 1952.

Martin, C. "But how do books help children?" *Junior Libraries*, 1955, *1*, 83-87.

Mattera, C. "Bibliotherapy in a sixth grade." Unpublished doctoral dissertation, Pennsylvania State University, 1961.

McCarthy, P., Gillotey, L., & Wagner, G. "Let's get together." *Education*, 1963, *83*, 564-566.

McCracken, C., & Walcutt, C. *Basic reading.* Philadelphia: Lippincott, 1963.

McLuhan, M. *The medium is the message.* New York: Random House, 1967.

Namnum, A., & Prelinger, E. "On the psychology of the reading process." *American Journal of Orthopsychiatry*, 1961, *31*, 820-827.

Panel Report. "The latency period." *Journal of the American Psychoanalytic Association*, 1957, *5*, 525-538.

Pearson, G. H. "A Survey of learning difficulties." *Psychoanalytic Study of the Child*, 1952, *7*, 322-386.

Peller, L. "Reading and daydreams in latency, boy-girl differences." *Journal of the American Psychoanalytic Association*, 1958, *6*, 57-70.

Whipple, G. *Appraisal of the city schools' reading program.* Detroit: Detroit Public Schools Division for Improvement of Instruction, Language Education Department, 1963.

Witty, P. A. "Meeting developmental needs through reading." *Education*, 1964, *84*, 451-458.

Zimet, S. G. "Children's interest and story preferences: a critical review of the literature." *Elementary School Journal*, 1966, *67*, 122-130.

CHAPTER 3

WHAT CHILDREN CHOOSE TO READ AND WHAT THEY HAVE TO READ

J. Lawrence Wiberg and Marion Trost

Numerous studies on children's reading preferences have been reported, of which only a few deal specifically with the reading interests of the first grade student. In a recent review of the literature (Zimet, 1966), it was pointed out that the reading preferences of young children change over time as society changes; that the research has neglected to investigate the reading interests of the beginning reader; and that there has been a tendency to infer reading interests of the younger child from research done with older children. Results of existing studies are confusing; they are contradictory or their methods are not comparable. For example, in one study, the reading interests of 275 first grade students were assessed using a questionnaire technique requiring "like" or "not like" answers (Rogers & Robinson, 1963). From rank order

This chapter first appeared, in its original version, as: Wiberg, J. L., and Trost, M. "Comparison of Content of First Grade Primers and Free Choice Library Selections," *Elementary English,* 48:792-98, 1970. Copyright © 1970 by the National Council of Teachers of English. Reprinted by permission of the publisher and J. Lawrence Wiberg and Marion Trost.

listings, differences were found in boy's and girl's preferences and, in general, there was a preference for entertaining as opposed to informational material. Another study (Byers, 1964), using a sharing session technique (small group discussions with teacher and pupils) with 1,860 first grade students from differing socioeconomic classes, revealed a preference for science and nature as compared to entertaining content. Sex preferences were demonstrated. A study of first graders free choice library selections (Smith, 1962) concluded that there was a preference for humor, fantasy, animals, nature and science, and that these categories were not well represented in preprimer and primer stories. In none of the above-mentioned studies were tests of statistical significance applied to the data.

The compiled data from the systematic objective analysis of story content found in primary reading textbook series currently in use in the United States have been reported in Chapter 1. In general, the authors were impressed by the restrictedness and inappropriateness of primer content in relation to the developmental interests of the first grade child. An extreme discrepancy was found between the actual lives of children and what is depicted in the story content. There was a predominance of poorly defined sex roles, an emphasis on middle-class suburban settings, themes of a pollyannaish quality, regressive emphases, and a tendency to denigrate the masculine role.

Subsequently, attention was turned toward considering the content of first graders' free choice library selections, assuming this would more closely reveal the natural reading interests and needs of the child. It was felt that it would be valuable to compare the primer content, with which the child is forced to deal in learning to read, and the content of his free choice library selections. To this end, the scheme of textbook content analysis was applied to a public school library selection designated for use by first grade students. A statistically reliable comparison between groups of primers and library books was carried out to test the following four hypotheses:

1. The story content of a group of first grade library books would differ significantly from the story content of a group of primer series.
2. In the library selection there would be significant differences in content between books "checked out" and "not checked out."
3. Although the groups of stories (library and primer) might be inherently different, as suggested by the first hypothesis, the books checked out in the

library selection would emphasize the differences between children's reading interests and what is presented in the primers.
4. Boy-girl differences would exist in content preferences in the free choice library selection.

METHOD

The national sample of primers was comprised of 1,307 stories in twelve of the most commonly used publishing series (Hollins, 1955). The library sample consisted of 639 books from the library of a middle- to upper-middle-class suburban elementary public school. There were 595 books on a free-standing shelf designated by the teachers and librarian for use by the first grade students; 44 nonfiction informational books were shelved elsewhere in the library, according to subject matter. Forty-five first grade students (23 boys and 22 girls) in two coeducational classes, went to the library for two periods a week during the academic year covered by this study. As is customary in the school, the students were required to check out one book per library period in the first six weeks of school, two per period in the second six weeks, then as many as they were interested in reading. In no way did this study interfere with the routine procedures of the library period. A complete record of each child's selection was kept. If a book was checked out more than once by the same child, it was counted as being checked out only once so that the findings would not be strongly influenced by a few children who might continue to select the same book.

The same coding manual developed for rating the primer stories, described in Chapter 1, was used in rating the library books. One rater coded the library sample, treating each book as one story. Intermittent re-tests with the other raters for reliability were consistently 90 percent or better.

Three distinct groups of stories were thus available for comparison: the national sample of primers and the library sample which was separated into checked-out and not-checked-out groups. A dimension by dimension, two-by-two table chi-square comparison was carried out between the three populations. Within the library checked-out group, it was also possible to look for significant differences in boy's and girl's selections.

RESULTS

Of 595 fiction books on the first grade shelf, 374 were checked out one or more times. Forty-four nonfiction informational books were checked out, indicating some exploratory activity on the part of the student as these books were scattered throughout other shelves. Boys and girls together checked out books 1,371 times. Boys checked out fiction books 580 times and information books 55 times; girls checked out fiction books 729 times and information books 7 times. The boys'

Table 3-1
**Significant Differences in Content between
National Sample and Library Sample (p $<$ .05)**

	National Sample	*Library Sample*
Character	Children Only	Make-Believe
	Children and Mother	Animals Only
	Children and Father	Inanimate Objects
	Children and Other Adults	
Theme	Active Play	Folk Tales
	Imaginative Play	Lessons from Life
	Pets	Nature
	Real Life with Positive Affect	Real Life with Negative Affect
Age	4-5 Years	6-7 Years
		10-11 Years
Sex	Girl	Boy
	Boy-Girl	
Outcome	Failure	Success
		Help
		Uncertain
Environment	Suburban	Urban
		Rural
		Make-Believe
		Other (foreign country, seashore, etc.)

preference for information books is significant (p <.001). The appendix contains a list by rank order of the 71 books most frequently checked out of the library.

Before considering specific differences between primers and library books, the previously stated four hypotheses will be considered individually.

Hypothesis 1: The story content of a group of first grade library books would demonstrably differ from the story content of a group of primer stories (see Table 3-1). The data strongly supports this hypothesis. The *p* value refers to a chi-square comparison between primer and library populations for each element of the six dimensions. For example, in the *character* dimension, there are significantly more stories (Primer Sample) with Children Only, Children and Mother, Children and Father, and Children and Other Adults, and this is contrasted in the table with the library sample where stories contained more Animals Only, Make-Believe, and Inanimate Objects. As is seen in looking at Table 3-1 as a whole, there is a marked disparity in content variables between the primer sample and library sample in all six dimensions.

Hypothesis 2: In the library sample there would be a significant difference in content between books checked out and books not checked out (see Table 3-2). Table 3-2 indicates that the data supports Hypothesis 2. Content preferences between the checked-out and

Table 3-2
**Differences in Content Between Books Checked
Out and Not Checked Out in Library Sample**

	Checked Out	*Not Checked Out*
Character	Make-Believe Animals Only	Children Only
Theme	Folk Tales Pranks	Outings Real Life with Positive Affect
Sex	Girl Activity	Boy-Girl Activity
Outcome	Failure	—
Environment	Make-Believe	Not Clear

not-checked-out books are present in five of the six categories. Of the checked-out books, no statistical differences in content could be demonstrated between the most frequently and least frequently checked-out books, e.g., the ten most checked out versus the ten least checked out.

Hypothesis 3: Although the groups of stories (library sample and primer sample) might be inherently different, the books checked out in the library selection would emphasize the difference between children's reading interests and what is presented in the primer series. Content differences between the primer sample and the checked-out segment of the library sample were present, but nearly identical to the differences between primer sample and total library sample. Hypothesis 3 is not supported; children's selectivity did not bring out new content differences. Checked-out books were characteristic of the library sample as a whole in terms of a comparison to the primer sample.

Hypothesis 4: Boy-girl differences would exist in content preferences in the free choice library selection (see Table 3-3). Evidence from the data for this hypothesis is not very strong. It is suggested that inanimate objects are preferred by both girls and boys. Boys prefer Boy activities, but girls have no preference for either Boy or Girl activities. Girls prefer stories about pets, boys about pranks and information, e.g., how-to-do-it books, books about fire engines, spaceships, etc.

Table 3-3
**Significant Boy-Girl Differences in Content
Preferences in Library Sample**

	Boy	Girl	Boy-Girl
Character	—	—	Inanimate
Theme	Information Pranks	Pets	—
Sex	Boy	—	—

DISCUSSION

Having given general consideration to the data supporting or not supporting the four hypotheses and the check-out frequency of the library sample, it seems best for purposes of discussion to look at comparative data dimension by dimension in the content analysis.

Character

The results indicate that the national sample is skewed towards child and child-adult interactions, while the library sample is weighted toward Animals Only, Make-Believe, and Inanimate Object characters (Table 3-1). Within the library sample (Table 3-2) there is a significant preference (checked-out) for Animals Only and Make-Believe and a non-preference (not-checked-out) for Children Only. Therefore, it appears that authors of children's library books are aware of the child's interest and need for fantasy-promoting material. This is also reflected by the librarian's selection of books for the first grade shelf. In contrast, make-believe characters are seldom seen in primers. Furthermore, primers, as measured by the national sample, overemphasize common day-to-day parent-child interaction and, perhaps unwittingly, take much of the interest and fun out of reading. The higher representation of Animals Only in the library sample and the child's corresponding preferences for this characterization points to an interest in living, feeling objects, not necessarily human.

Sex preferences regarding characters is interestingly demonstrated in that stories popular to both boys and girls have a significantly higher population of inanimate objects (Table 3-3). Reasons are not obvious, even after closer inspection of the stories. We can only speculate that the asexual nature of inanimate objects do not attract or repel boys or girls to give a sex-linked expression of preference.

Theme

The national sample presents predominantly happy here-and-now play activities. In contrast, the library sample dealt more often with folk tales and showed no hesitancy to moralize or delve into unhappy feelings around unpleasant situations. There was also a stronger representation of nature. Children indicated a preference for the tradition and imagery of folk tales. Pranks, as a preferred theme, appear to reflect a satisfaction of the child's need to manipulate, scheme, and perhaps deceive, often with surprising and occasionally unhappy outcomes. That "outings" fell into the not-checked-out group is somewhat paradoxical in view of a common impression that children delight in such activity. Inspection of those stories revealed that many center around child-adult or parent-child interaction which, as previously seen, were not particularly well-represented or popular characters in the library sample. Real life with positive affect was also in the not-checked-out group. The child's experience tells him that happiness is not a constant, dependable phenomenon. A steady, unrelieved diet of positive affect does not characterize a child's real life experience. One wonders if the child avoids this theme because it predominates in the primers.

Informational books were strongly preferred by boys. This deserves further comment. As mentioned, it was necessary for the child to explore the library to select this type of book. This exploratory activity, done mostly by boys, is one indication of the first grade boy's more general need to familiarize himself with the "what and how" of worldly phenomenon (Kagan, 1964). Certainly this is in part culturally determined: the male is expected to seek out, assimilate, and use knowledge to cope with his environment in a way that provides for his family's well-being. This is already a life task for the first grade boy (Erikson, 1950). The boy's preference for pranks suggests that the previously speculated child's need to manipulate, scheme, and deceive is experienced more by boys and is linked to feelings of anticipation and humor often associated with daring behavior.

Age

Differences in age of activity were present in the comparison of the national sample to the library sample. The primer sample was skewed toward an age distribution less than that of the first grade child (four to five years). The age distribution of the library sample centered around two groups, the first being the appropriate first grade age range of six to seven years. The second group, the ten to eleven year range, presents situations and activities toward which a child can strive. Such stories imply greater mastery over and more involved interaction with the environment. This is in distinct contrast to the regressive age pull of primer stories.

Sex

Girl activity and Boy-Girl activity exist in greater proportion in the primer sample, whereas Boy activity predominates in the library sample. In our previous study of the national sample, the loading of Girl activity and Boy-Girl activity stories were noted and discussed. In particular, it was felt there was distinct ambiguity in sex role in relation to the activities depicted (see Chap. 1). In examining the checked-out versus the not-checked-out sample, it is seen that Boy-Girl activity was significantly higher in the not-checked-out segment. This would lend credibility to the speculation that ambiguity in sex role is avoided by the child. Girl activities characterized the checked-out group, which is probably related to the fact that girls checked out more books than boys. It has been generally documented that girls read more than boys (Gray, 1960), and this applied to our pupil population as reflected by the number of times books were checked out.

Boys preferred Boy activity stories, whereas girls showed no preference as to the sex of activity. The reason for the latter case is not immediately apparent. We do know, however, that the home and school environment of the first grade boy is predominantly feminine at a time when he feels a greater need for masculine contacts and activities. This may be partially met by reading Boy activity stories. Establishing a feminine identification for the girl is less difficult in the first grade setting; there is no need to seek out Girl activity stories.

Outcome

Failure as outcome predominated in the primer sample. The library sample was skewed toward Success, Help, and Uncertain. Interestingly, the checked-out portion of the library sample indicated a preference for Failure. On a first impression, the quality of failure differed between the national sample and the checked-out portion of the library sample. The stereotyped Failure in the national sample more often resulted from ignorance, incompetence, or negligence. Failure in the library sample stemmed from adventuresome, daring types of activities where the character was more directly responsible for the outcome, or could not realistically be expected to accomplish the given activity. Negative affect accompanied Failure outcome in the library sample and was also more clearly and realistically depicted—a smiling face was not the response to a broken toy!

Environment

The primer sample routinely presents a green lawn, white picket fence, and other stereotypes of the suburban environment. In comparison to the national sample, the library sample provides a much richer selection of environmental settings. There seems to be no inherent advantage in the extensive use of stereotypes as opposed to diversity in any educational venture. The content of primers is no exception. Certainly children from lower socioeconomic groups would have difficulty identifying with the primer sample stereotype. Regardless of socioeconomic class, the range of environments in the library sample presents higher motivational content in meeting the child's desire to enjoy, explore, inform, and master. In looking at what was checked out and not checked out, it can be seen that a make-believe environment was distinctly popular. This, of course, correlates with a previously noted preference for make-believe characters. "Not clear" environments were representative of the not-checked-out books. Again, it may be inferred that the child needs to place reading content into an identifiable frame of reference, be it real life or clearly labeled and permissible make-believe.

DISCUSSION

In this study we have attempted to separate and discuss individual elements in stories. In Chapter 1, a general Gestalt for the primer stories was described. It is more difficult to describe a Gestalt for a "typical" library story. These stories are not predictably stereotyped. We feel this is a virtue. They tend to cluster into two groups: (1) those with fun, fantasy, highly creative imagery, plot, and characterization, and (2) those with adventure, age-appropriateness or relevance to a more advanced age, information, and life-oriented realism. A gross distinction is evident between primer stories and the selection of library stories reported here.

REFERENCES

Byers, L. "Pupils' interests and the content of primary reading texts." *The Reading Teacher*, 1964, *17*, 227-233.

Erikson, E. *Childhood and society*. New York: Norton, 1950.

Gray, W. S. "Physiology and psychology of reading." In the *Encyclopedia of Educational Research*, 3rd ed. New York: Macmillan, 1960, pp. 1096-1114.

Hollins, W. H. "A national survey of commonly used first grade readers." Unpublished data, Alabama A & M College, 1955.

Kagan, J. "Acquisition and significance of sex typing and sex role identity." In M. L. Hoffman & L. W. Hoffman (Eds.), *Child development research*. Vol. 1. New York: Russell Sage Foundation, 1964, pp. 137-166.

Rogers, H., & Robinson, H. A. "Reading interests of the first grader." *Elementary English*, 1963, *40*, 707-711.

Smith, R. C. "Children's reading choices and basic reader content." *Elementary English*, 1962, *39*, 202-209.

Witty, P., Coomer, A., & McBean, D. "Children's choices of favorite books: a study conducted in ten elementary schools." *Journal of Educational Psychology*, 1946, *37*, 266-278.

Zimet, S. G. "Children's interests and story preferences." *Elementary School Journal*, 1966, *67*, 122-130.

CHAPTER 4

CHILDREN'S PREFERENCES

Cynthia Rose, Sara G. Zimet, and Gaston E. Blom

It has been proposed by Fred Busch in Chapter 2, that first graders will prefer reading textbook story content that deals with issues that are of developmental concern and interest to first grade children. The study discussed in this chapter sets out to determine whether this is actually the case.

The library selection study discussed in Chapter 3 indicated that first grade children preferred stories with pranks as a theme, activities appropriate to seven- to nine-year-olds and activities that had the same gender association as the child reading the story, that is, boys preferred reading about boy-associated activities and girls preferred reading about girl-associated activities. The authors of Chapter 1 also designated peer interaction and successful outcome stories as developmentally pertinent issues for first graders. Thus the following hypotheses evolved:

This chapter first appeared, in its original version, as: Rose, C., Zimet, S. G., and Blom, G. E. "Content Counts: Children Have Preferences in Reading Textbook Stories," *Elementary English*, January, 1972 (in press). Reprinted by permission of the National Council of Teachers of English.

1. First grade children prefer reading textbook stories with pranks as a theme as opposed to a Pollyanna theme.
2. First grade children prefer reading textbook stories with activities rated as older than six-year-old children rather than with activities rated as younger than six-year-old children.
3. First grade children prefer reading textbook stories with peer interaction only to stories with parent-child interaction.
4. First grade boys prefer reading textbook stories with Boy activities to stories with Girl activities.
5. First grade girls prefer reading textbook stories with girl-activity to boy-activity stories.
6. First grade children prefer reading textbook stories with success outcome to failure outcome.

METHOD

Several investigators (Emans, 1968; Emans & Walz, 1969; Rankin, 1968; Rogers & Robinson, 1963) had established that younger children can indicate content preference when given age-appropriate methods of responding.

Subjects

Seventy-six first graders from two middle-class suburban public elementary schools were subjects for this study. There were 41 boys and 35 girls. The study was conducted during the second half of the school year.

Selection of Stories

A pool of 117 primary level stories were chosen from the 1,307 stories coded in a national sample (Waite et al., 1967; Blom, Waite, & Zimet, 1968) and these were computerized. The computer selected out pairs of stories held constant for length, reading difficulty level, environmental setting, and other identified content factors except for each single variable being tested in the above-stated hypotheses. The content variables selected for comparison within each pair of stories are shown in Table 4-1.

Table 4-1

Selected Content Variables in Stories
from Primary Reading Textbooks

General Content Factor	Story Pair	Content Variable
Theme	A	Pranks
		Pollyanna
Activity Age	B	Younger age activity (3-5 years)
		Older age activity (7-9 years)
Character Interaction	C	Peer interaction
		Parent and child interaction
Sex of Activity	D	Boy activity
		Girl activity
Activity Outcome	E	Success
		Failure

Procedures

Five selected pairs of stories (See Table 4-1) were read to groups of from six to thirteen children. As each page of the story was read, it was simultaneously projected onto a large screen in front of the group. All ten stories were read in one sitting.

Immediately after each pair of stories was presented and read, the children were asked to indicate on their individual answer sheets which story they preferred. The entire session with each group took a total of 35 minutes to complete.

The order of presentation of each set of stories was reversed with each new group of children in both schools to control for order effect. The same adult read the stories to all groups in both schools to eliminate the influence of the personality of the reader on the subjects.

Six children were selected at random, three from each school, for a follow-up inquiry as to why they preferred the stories they selected. Each of these six children was interviewed separately by the same adult who read the stories, and the interviews were taperecorded.

FINDINGS

Story preferences were noted for each pair of stories. The binomial test was used to identify significant differences in selection within pairs for the total group of first grade subjects.

As shown in Table 4-2, Hypotheses 1 and 3 were supported by the data for the total group. There was a significant (p<.05) preference for

Table 4-2

Frequency of Preference Shown Between Story Pairs by Total Group of 76 First Graders

Story Pair	Content Variable	Frequency of Preference
A	Pranks	62
	Pollyanna	14
B	Younger age activity	40
	Older age activity	36
C	Peer interaction	59
	Child and parent interaction	17
D	Boy activity	37
	Girl activity	39
E	Success	38
	Failure	39

the pranks theme over the pollyanna theme (Pair A) and for the peer interaction story over the child and parent interaction story (Pair C). No significant preference trend was discernible in the categories of younger activity versus older activity (Pair B) or success outcome versus failure outcome (Pair E). Thus, Hypotheses 2 and 6 were not supported by data for the total group.

Hypotheses 4 and 5 were confirmed when the subjects were separated according to sex. Table 4-3 (Pair D) shows that boys prefer the Boy story and that girls prefer the Girl story (χ^2 = 12.5, p<.001). Both girls and boys show a significant story preference for pranks over Pollyanna (p<.001, Pair A) and peer interaction over child and parent interaction (p<.001, Pair C). With the younger activity story versus older activity story (Pair B), and success outcome versus failure outcome stories (Pair E), boys and girls showed no significant preference trend. When examined according to sex differences, Hypotheses 1, 3, 4, and 5 were supported. Hypotheses 2 and 6 were not.

Table 4-3

Boy and Girl Preferences of Story Pairs

		Frequency of Preference	
Story Pair	*Content Variable*	*Boys (N=41)*	*Girls (N=35)*
A	Pranks	31	31
	Pollyanna	10	4
B	Younger activity	22	18
	Older activity	19	17
C	Peer interaction	33	26
	Child and parent interaction	8	9
D	Boy activity	28	9
	Girl activity	13	26
E	Success	20	18
	Failure	21	17

To test the order effect of the stories, a binominal test was applied. No significant difference appeared. The selection of stories was not influenced by the order of their presentation.

Attempts to have the six randomly selected children identify the reasons for their story preference through individual interviews met with random and idiosyncratic responses. The children reported reactions to aspects of a story other than those under investigation. For example, one child preferred a story that reminded him of his veiled interest in seeing his younger brother abandoned. The story had an illustration of a young boy alone in a boat. Another child projected onto a story character, a dog. Here the dog triggered the child's memory of a real-life episode where her dog saved her family's life. A third child simply commented, "The author has a very good style. I like the way he writes." Therefore it is unclear whether children of this age are cognitively capable of verbally reporting their rationale for story preference or whether the investigators' method was not appropriately structured for collection of a measurable verbal report in relation to the dimensions studied.

DISCUSSION

The choice of a pranks theme over a Pollyanna theme (Pair A) and peer interaction over child-parent interaction (Pair C) indicates a definite content preference by first graders. It is interesting to note that the group choice of stories with a pranks theme over a Pollyanna theme is in direct contrast to the relative availability of these themes in primary reading textbooks. Out of 1,307 textbook stories in the national sample coded for theme, 23 percent were rated Pollyanna and only 3 percent were rated pranks (Blom, et al., 1967). In Pair C where the total group and boys and girls separately preferred peer interaction over parent-child interaction stories, the first grade textbook content analysis again showed a dearth of such stories. Coding revealed that 38.5 percent of the 1,307 stories presented parent-child interaction while only 11 percent dealt with peer interaction (Blom et al., 1967).

The developmental relevance of the textbook story content, as defined by these investigators, coincides with the children's story preferences. These preferences represent motivational forces for facilitating the first grader's initial approach to reading instruction. Textbook authors and publishers should give consideration to increasing the frequency of inclusion of pranks themes and peer interaction stories in primary reading textbooks.

In this study, boys preferred Boy stories and girls preferred Girl stories. When the availability of such stories in primary reading materials was examined, there were 25.7 percent Boy stories and 28.3 percent Girl stories. The remaining 46 percent of the 1,307 stories rated were classified as diffuse on this dimension, i.e., appropriate for boys and girls together (Blom et al., 1967). Researchers have established that ambiguity of sex role is more appropriate for the preschool age child (Kagan, 1964). However, it is not clear what preferences first grade children would indicate towards sex ambiguous activity stories. While the investigators' findings indicate that textbook authors and publishers should continue including clearly identifiable boy- and girl-related activities in first grade reading textbooks, the necessity exists for further exploration of whether there is a preference for stories with diffuse sex of activities.

The results of this study indicated that there was no preference for either younger or older age activities (Pair B). It can be conjectured that the first grader will respond positively to a story with older age activity. This story would serve as an instructive socializing model. Yet the first grade children in this study preferred the younger activity story as frequently as they chose the older activity story. Older activity models can be growth-promoting and developmentally pertinent. At any one point in time, however, first graders can relate equally positively to regressive models (the story with a younger activity level). The distribution of age of activities in first grade reading textbooks (the national sample) was: two- to five-year-old activities, 40 percent; six- to seven-year-old activities, 47 percent; eight- to nine-year-old activities, 17 percent; and over ten-year-old activities, 1 percent. There is a need for balancing the distribution of older activities in first grade reading textbooks.

There was also no clear-cut preference for success outcome over failure outcome (Pair C). It may be that the quality of the outcome, that is, how believable or meaningful was the achievement of the success or the occurrence of failure, as well as the affects associated with the outcome, had as much or more influence on the child's story preference as the valence of the outcome. Controls for the quality of the handling of the success and failure outcome stories was not built into this investigation. Further study is needed.

Aside from Pair A, the quality of handling the story material, that is, plausibility of the plot, the nature of the interaction between characters, and the affect related to the activities, has not been considered in depth. The demonstrated positive story preference findings are not any the less valid, but this does indicate the need for further investigation and delineation of content factors in first grade reading textbooks. There are also implications for further study of the potential effect on learning to read by using children's preferred content in primary reading textbooks.

This study reports story content preferences of first grade children using only a single pair of stories for each of the five general content factors—theme, age of activity, character interaction, sex of activity, and outcome of activity. While significant findings exist, a larger number of paired stories for each content factor, rather than a single pair, would provide a more adequate sampling on which generalizations could be made. It should also be noted that the stories were read to the children. The findings might have been different had the children read the stories themselves.

First grade is a crucial year on the child's road to reading. The signals he perceives can establish a stop, wait, or go pattern and influence his speed limit. Poor reading has long been labeled as a cause of many educational and social ills. It is important to present the beginning reader with all the possible positive motivating factors. While method and format are important, content counts too!

REFERENCES

Blom, G. E., Waite, R. R., & Zimet, S. G. Unpublished data collected for content analysis study, University of Colorado Medical Center, Denver, Colorado, 1967.

Emans, R. "What do children in the inner city like to read?" *Elementary School Journal*, 1968, *49*, 119-122.

Emans, R., & Walz, C. A. "For beginning readers: what kinds of materials." *Elementary School Journal*, 1969, *70*, 91-98.

Kagan, J. "Acquisition and significance of sex typing and sex role identity." In M. L. Hoffman and L. W. Hoffman (eds.), *Review of child development research*. New York: Russell Sage Foundation, 1964, pp. 137-167.

Rankin. E. F., & Thames, C. L. "A methodology for studying children's reactions to stories in first grade readers." *Reading Teacher*, 1968, *22*, 242-245.

Rogers, H., & Robinson, H. A. "Reading interests of first graders" *Elementary English*, 1963, *60*, 707-711.

Waite, R. R., Blom, G. E., Zimet, S. G., & Edge, S. "First grade reading textbooks." *Elementary School Journal*, 1967, *67*, 336-374.

CHAPTER 5

AN ATTEMPT
TO RACIALLY INTEGRATE
AND URBANIZE A FIRST GRADE
READING TEXTBOOK

Gaston E. Blom, Richard R. Waite and Sara G. Zimet

Klineberg (1963) has referred to the picture of American society as presented in primers as being exclusively white, and its people being Northern European in appearance and origin. Southern Europeans are presented most frequently in stereotypes. There are some references to dark-skinned people who live in far away places, but "Negroes are nonexistent." In terms of these characteristics as well as others, Klineberg surmizes that such readers have an alien quality for a great many children. He contrasts the readers with a Brazilian first reader which tells children that Brazil has three mothers, one European—white, one Indian—red, and one African—black.

Fischer (1966) further amplifies the need for improved textbooks for white and black children.

This chapter first appeared, in its original version, as: Blom, G. E., Waite, R. R., and Zimet, S. G. "Ethnic Integration and Urbanization of A First Grade Reading Textbook: A Research Study," *Psychology in the Schools*, 4: 176-181, 1967.

The areas of textbooks and other teaching materials is also enormously important today. I could argue that perhaps the greater importance, if there is to be a comparison made, is the development of materials for white children rather than for Negro children. Usually the argument is that we need better material for Negro children in order to give them self-respect. Of course we need them. But we also need materials for the white children, who have been very badly misinformed about the whole business of racial groups (pp. 419-420).

Larrick (1965) indicates that more than six million nonwhite children are learning to read in books which omit them. There is a blatant racial bias not only in textbooks but tradebooks too have almost completely omitted blacks. In a survey of over 5,000 children's tradebooks in a three-year period (1962-1965) less than 7 percent included one or more blacks. There has been no significant percentage increase over these years in spite of the recent pressure of the civil rights movement. Larrick states that even where blacks appeared in books they were most frequently placed outside the United States or at a time period before World War II. The word black or Negro was seldom used and black characters were depicted in common stereotypes.

With one exception (Michalak, 1965), the few multiethnic readers which are currently published have been criticized for being similar to the usual basal readers except for the skin color of the characters (Dolmatch, 1965), being "Dick-and-Jane bound," and having a limited vocabulary (Green & Ryan, 1966; Hechinger, 1965). Given the deficiencies in such developments, one point of view is that current integrated textbooks and classroom supplements of books and bulletins that focus on minority groups are modest milestones and are a bridge to eventually fully integrated textbooks (Newsweek, 1966).

The study presented here is a content analysis of the 118 stories in a multiethnic urban first grade reading series which was published first in 1962 and completed in 1964. This particular series was carefully constructed with the idea that children in urban situations could more readily identify with story characters that represented the types of people seen in multicultural neighborhoods (Marburger, 1963; Whipple, 1964). The stories and illustrations were designed to develop suspense, surprise, humor, and high interest. Natural familiar speech patterns in word usage were employed. The vocabulary was carefully chosen with large numbers of active verbs. Whipple (1964) compared this series with a widely used one in terms of interest appeal, preferences, and reading acquisition, using as subjects a biracial group of children in varied socioeconomic and cultural neighborhoods. The results clearly favored the urban series. However, the question could be raised whether the initial favorable results are based upon the influence of enthusiasm, newness, and other attitudes (Hawthorne effect).

METHOD

The procedures used for these ratings have been described in Chapter 1. Agreements among raters on the ratings of the dimensions in the urban series were 84 percent.

The results of the urban series content analysis were compared to those of the national sample of commonly used primers (12 series, 1,307 stories) for both differences and similarities in content. Some further analyses focused specifically on ethnic issues. A number of qualitative characteristics were discerned which could not be quantified, as were the other dimensions of the content analysis.

RESULTS

Theme and Character Ratings

The frequency distributions of the themes depicted in the urban series strikingly parallel those in the national sample of all-white stories in common use today. Stories classified as Real Life Situations With Positive Affect are most frequent in both groups of stories. A noteworthy difference is that the distribution of characters in the urban series stories shows a greater emphasis on family groups than is found in the national sample. Whereas 38 percent of the stories in the national sample showed children with one or both parents, 57 percent of the stories in the urban series contained these constellations of characters. Thus, the theme and character ratings indicate that the urban series contains a somewhat exaggerated perpetuation of the stereotypical family-centered, pollyannaish, and bland activities.

Age of Activities

The ratings of age of activity for the urban series were compared with those for the national sample. The urban series contained a greater proportion of activities rated as being appropriate to children of more than six years than did the national sample. However, the difference between the two was not statistically significant.

Sex of Activity Ratings

The ratings of sex of activity for the urban series result in a frequency distribution similar to that of the national sample. In both groups about half of the story activities are rated as being appropriate for both sexes (Boy-Girl ratings), with the remainder split fairly evenly between the sexes.* When the raters were asked to place each Boy-Girl story into one sex category or the other whenever possible, their forced choices divided evenly between the sexes in both the urban series and the national sample.

Attributes of Characters—Age, Sex, and Family

Ratings on the characters in the stories based on their pictorial representations, as distinguished from the sex and age appropriateness of the activities, revealed two differences between the groups of stories. First, in the urban series there is a greater frequency of stories with family and nonfamily members together than in the national sample. In other words, children from outside the family are more frequently included in the stories. Second, the typical family constellation in the national sample includes the parents, a boy and a girl, each about six years old, and a younger sister. In the urban series, the typical family is similar, except that a younger brother replaces the younger sister.

Outcome Ratings

The ratings of outcome of activities revealed striking differences between the urban series and the national sample. First, the urban

---

*The actual percentages on original sex of activity ratings were: national sample, 45 percent, and urban series, 52 percent for Boy-Girl ratings.

stories' activities end in failure nearly twice as frequently as they end in success, which is in marked contrast to the national sample. Second, in the urban series, there are about as many activities which end in Help, as in Success.* In the national sample, seven times as many stories end in Success as in Help. The differences between the two distributions are statistically significant (p <.001). Moreover, none of the twelve series in the national sample contains more Failure stories than Success stories, nor do any of them contain such a high proportion of Help stories. Thus, the urban series is distinctly different from all of the other series we have studied, i.e., it is different from those most frequently used by schools in this country.

Environmental Setting Ratings

The stories were rated according to the environmental setting in which they occurred: Urban, Suburban, Rural, Not Clear, and Other (make-believe, foreign countries, etc.). The results on the urban series indicate that Suburban settings predominate to even a larger degree than in the national sample although there are more Urban stories and fewer Rural stories.

Ethnicity Ratings

The final rating of the stories in the urban series, that of ethnic character, was carried out to determine the extent to which characters from Negro, Caucasian, and other races appear in the stories. The results indicate no particular relationship between the two dimensions, suggesting that the preponderance of Failure stories is a general phenomenon characteristic of this series, and is not correlated to the presence or absence of particular racial groups.

DISCUSSION

The ratings of theme, character attributes, and sex and age appropriateness of activities provide results which would indicate that

*A story is rated Help if the main activity is completed only with the assistance of a helping person, usually a parent.

in many ways the urban series closely approximates the other series used by schools. The environmental setting of the stories is even more suburban than the national sample. These results suggest that the urban series is essentially no different from the other series, except for the ethnic composition of characters. Qualitative examination of the stories reveals that what is actually being depicted is a black family living in a happy, stable, white, suburban neighborhood. No blacks other than members of the primary family appear. The original aims of the group which wrote these primers were "to build a series of pre-primers which would focus on the life of a working-class family, living in a typical, racially mixed, urban neighborhood" (Marburger, 1963, p. 305). Marburger has pointed out that these aims were frustrated by a variety of factors, and the results of the content analysis reported here indicate the degree of that frustration.

A striking major difference between the urban series and other publishers' series examined is in the outcome of the activities depicted in the stories. Because the ratio of Failure to Success in this series is so strikingly different from that in other stories, it is important to review and understand exactly what these ratings focus on. The outcome of a story is rated Success if the main activity depicted in the story is carried out by the characters to the point where they accomplish that which they set out to do. An example of Success is when in the beginning of a story some children attempt to fly a kite and at its conclusion the kite is flying. A story is rated as Failure if the main activity ends without the goal of that activity being accomplished. For example, if the children attempt to fly the kite and the family dog becomes entangled in the string, causing the kite to fall, a rating of Failure would be made. Stories are rated Help if the characters engaged in the activity are unable to succeed in that activity, but another character, usually an adult, enters the activity and assists them in accomplishing their goal. If the children could not fly the kite, and their father comes onto the scene and is responsible for getting it to fly, the story would be rated Help.

Of the 118 stories in the urban series, 61 depicted an activity in which the characters began a goal-directed activity and failed to attain that goal. In 23 stories the goal was reached only with the assistance of an adult after an initial failure. In only 33 stories, less than one-third of the total, were children depicted as being entirely successful in achieving their goal.

The question of whether or not the variables studied in this investigation affect the rate at which children learn to read is one which awaits empirical findings. "It has long been felt that children might read with greater facility if the material with which they were dealing was more related to their own real backgrounds" (Marburger, 1963, p. 305). "Needed: a book written from stories by the children of Harlem, beautifully illustrated, about a real child in Harlem who experiences some kind of success. Everyone agrees on this. But we still do not see such a basic reader in use in most schools" (Green & Ryan, 1966, p. 187). Clearly, other writers also believe that the content of the stories do have motivational value (Davis, 1965; Karey, 1966; Niemeyer, 1965; Whipple & Black, 1966).

If the hypothesis is valid that the development of reading skill is related to the content of the stories in reading textbooks, then the presentation of a preponderance of Failure stories raises questions about the appropriateness of the stories. The first story in the series is a case in point. It begins with a black child sitting down to read. Before he can open one of his books, a second child (white) tickles him, with the result that the black child drops his books and chases the white child. The story ends with absolutely no reading ever being accomplished.

Among the goals of the authors of the urban series was the aforementioned wish to write stories focused on urban neighborhoods. This was clearly not accomplished. The authors were successful in presenting stories with characters of Negro, Caucasian, and other races. Another goal was to create success experiences for their young students by shortening the first preprimer so that "each child [could] have the satisfaction of completing a book in a short time" (Marburger, 1963, p. 305). This goal was apparently realized also. However, the results of this study indicate that in the process of meeting these goals, the authors created a series of stories which made it necessary for the children to focus their learning attention on the activities of a group of boys and girls who most of the time are unable to succeed in whatever they attempt to do, be it age-appropriate play or reading.

REFERENCES

Davis, A. "Teaching language and reading to disadvantaged Negro children." *Elementary English*, 1965, *42*, 791-797.

Dolmatch, T. B. "Color me brown—I'm integrated." *Saturday Review*, September 11, 1965, p. 73.

Fischer, J. H. "In Transcript of the American Academy Conference on the Negro American, May 14-15, 1965." *Daedalus*, 1966, *95*, 287-444.

Green, M. F., & Ryan, O. *The school children (Growing up in the slums).* New York: Random House, 1966.

Hechinger, F. M. "Better primers." *The New York Times*, January 24, 1965.

Karey, R. A. "Children's literature for integrated classes." *Elementary English*, 1966, *43*, 39-42.

Klineberg, O. "Life is fun in a smiling, fair-skinned world." *Saturday Review*, February 16, 1963, pp. 75-77.

Larrick, N. "The all-white world of children's books." *Saturday Review*, September 11, 1965, pp. 63-65, 84-85.

Marburger, C. L. "Considerations for educational planning." In A. H. Passow (ed.), *Education in depressed areas*. New York: Teachers College Press, 1963, pp. 298-321.

Michalak, J. "City life in primers." *Sunday New York Herald Tribune*, January 24, 1965.

"Integrating the Texts." *Newsweek*, March 7, 1966.

Niemeyer, J. H. "The Bank Street Readers: support for movement toward an integrated society." *The Reading Teacher,* 1965, *18,* 542-545.

Whipple, G. "Multicultural primers for today's children." *Education Digest*, 1964, *29*, 26-29.

Whipple, G., & Black, M. H. *Reading for children without—our dis-advantaged youth, reading aid series*. Newark, Del.: International Reading Association, 1966.

CHAPTER 6

BLACK AND WHITE FAMILIES IN A MULTIETHNIC URBAN PRIMER

Richard R. Waite

In 1962 a series of first grade reading textbooks was designed to meet the needs of pupils in multicultural neighborhoods (Whipple, 1963). These books included as characters a black family and a white boy from next door. Prior to 1962, black characters had been excluded from American primers. The authors of the series attempted to construct the books in ways which would provide children with feelings of accomplishment as soon as possible. The stories were designed to make more use of suspense and surprise endings than one usually finds in such books. The teacher's manual accompanying the series placed emphasis on social objectives as well as skill objectives since it was deemed urgent that all children develop proper attitudes toward others.

This chapter first appeared, in its original version, as: Waite, R. R., "Some Character Types in Negro Primers: A Psychoanalytic Study." Unpublished paper presented to the Denver Psychoanalytic Society, Denver, Colorado, February 1968. Reprinted by permission.

The series was introduced into selected classrooms. Measurements were obtained of the children's levels of word recognition, the accuracy of their oral reading, and the interest appeal of the books. The results were compared with those from classrooms that used traditional all-white books. In each case the new series was more effective. From interviews with the children it was concluded that the authors of the series were very successful in depicting characters with whom urban children can identify. In the words of a teacher, "the characters are alive and real to the children and the children in general show no racial discrimination in their reactions to the characters" (Whipple, 1963, p. 29).

In 1964 the series was completed with the addition of three more advanced books, which extended the range from the first preprimer to the final primer. In the last three books, the number of central characters was expanded to ten: the black family—father, mother, Jimmy (age six), Debbie (age six), and David (age four); a white family—father, mother, Larry (age six), and Suzy (age four); Linda, a six-year-old girl of Hispanic background; and Carlos, a six-year-old boy also of Hispanic background, who appears in a few stories at the end of the series.

The authors of the series explicitly state that the characters in the stories are to be conceptualized as identification figures who provide role models for the children. [We would agree that children should be encouraged to identify with the story characters. Such identification lends importance to our attempt to understand the characters further, and this is one of the reasons why the present study was attempted.]

The study of a multiethnic series of primers can provide more than an understanding of what children are being asked to read in school. The appearance of multiethnic primers on the educational scene within the past six years is but one of many efforts to make it possible for this country's minority group members to gain educational, social, political, and economic opportunities heretofore denied them. To a considerable extent, these efforts are directed toward the firm incorporation of middle-class values by lower-class people. Those who are responsible for the creation, development, and implementation of programs designed to achieve these aims are most frequently people from the middle class, either because of their birth or because of their own educational or economic achievements. Their programs express the conscious attitude that there are "no real differences" between blacks and whites. We would predict that, in attempting to portray situations in which blacks were equal to whites, the authors of these series suggest, in one way or another, differences between blacks and whites that are based more on cultural stereotypes than on objectively defined cultural attributes. Data from our previous studies strongly suggest that, despite their simplicity, primer stories do manifest a variety of ethnic attitudes and values. Statistical data concerning multiethnic primers indicate that conflicting attitudes toward minority group members are represented in the stories.

With these ideas in mind, comparisons of white and black characters were made. A comparison was first made of the two six-year-old boys, Jimmy and Larry. Upon superficial examination, these two boys appeared to differ only in respect to their race. No similar comparison was possible for girls since no six-year-old white girl was available for comparison with the black girl. One of the main interests in our studies of all primers is the manner in which masculine adequacy is represented in them. Therefore our attention then turned to the two fathers. Our data strongly suggest that the representation of masculine adequacy is one area in which authors frequently convey a distorted reflection of reality. The general presentation of the fathers is quite similar to the characterizations in television's situation comedies. The characterization of the paternal character in multiethnic primers is of utmost importance since he is intended to be a figure for identification and, as documented by Moynihan (1965), in many black families the father is absent. That the authors of the urban series were aware of the father's importance was revealed by the fact that they quoted one of the teachers who took part in their study as follows: "Father is presented as a strong character in the pre-primers. His role is well defined. There is a close relationship between father and the children. This is a very important factor since many of the children in our room are without fathers" (Whipple, 1963, p. 32).

The characters in this series of books are without surnames, so for convenience of identification the blacks in the book are referred to here as the "Black" family and their white neighbors as the "White" family.

Both families live in the suburbs in modest homes and go to a school which was built within the last fifteen years. Both own automobiles. They take trips to the park, the city, and the beach, usually in their automobiles but sometimes on the bus. The Black family has a nameless female cat and the White family owns a dog named Wiggles. We are not told the occupation of the boys' fathers, but the suburban environment in which they live suggests that they earn salaries equivalent at least to that of skilled tradesmen.

ANALYSIS OF JIMMY AND LARRY

The first four stories are continuous. They begin with Jimmy Black coming out of his house and sitting down on the front steps with several books, getting ready to read. Just as he begins, Larry White, who is hiding in a nearby bush, tickles Jimmy with a little branch. The first story ends as Jimmy drops the books and discovers Larry, who is trying rather unsuccessfully to contain his laughter. We then see Jimmy chasing Larry around the yard, both boys obviously enjoying themselves. As Larry runs back toward the steps, Debbie Black appears and, stepping in front of her brother, blocks his pursuit. Just then Larry reaches the steps, trips on the books and falls, cutting his knee. Saddened by this turn of events, Jimmy attempts to comfort his friend, and Debbie runs into the house to tell her mother about the accident.

In the third story we find Larry in the Black home receiving aid and comfort from Mrs. Black in the form of a red Band-Aid and a lollypop. In the fourth story, little David Black takes a box of colored Band-Aids and begins covering himself with them at random while Larry and Jimmy begin looking at the books. David is discovered by Larry, who takes delight in pointing out what the little boy is doing, whereupon everyone laughs at David's childishly inappropriate behavior.

These four stories provide considerable information about the two boys, how they differ, some of the ways in which they express their affects, and their reactions to environmental pressures. From these four stories we can derive several hypotheses about the behavioral characteristics of each boy.

The first hypothesis has to do with Jimmy Black's impulsiveness. Reading is a skill which most six-year-olds are capable of mastering and one our culture expects the children of this age to begin to attain. The reader's initial impression is that Jimmy is interested in this achievement. We could say that he is attuned to middle-class values. But how interested is he? One interruption, and he throws the books down and begins a new, more action-oriented activity, one which includes considerable more affective expression than cognitive effort. The initial guess then is that Jimmy is an impulsive child, easily distracted and not as strongly interested in learning.

Next there is the matter of Jimmy's expression of his aggressive drives through play. He apparently has the ego mechanisms necessary for the expression of aggression in accordance with reality considerations. That is, he chose a playful activity for getting back at Larry. Nevertheless, his behavior leads to destructive consequences and one would hypothesize that his ego mechanisms function appropriately in the face of aggressive wishes, but these wishes are likely to gain direct gratification and consequent loss of self-esteem.

Larry is also a boy who possesses the ego mechanisms necessary to express his aggression through developmentally appropriate channels. But he hurts himself in the process, suggesting a tendency for his aggression to be turned back upon himself. Next, he is hyperalert to the infantile behavior of Jimmy's brother. It could be that another characteristic way in which he expresses his aggression is through making fun of others, belittling them.

Several other hypotheses are possible. One gets the impression that Larry is the brighter, more alert, more inventive of the two boys. He is the one who fools Jimmy and he is the one who notices David's inappropriate use of the Band-Aids. He is the instigator of activities, not the follower. He may not be as physically well coordinated since he falls and is hurt. Finally, the fact that Jimmy's attempts to read are frustrated in part by external factors suggests the possibility that the world in which he lives is apt to make it difficult for him to achieve scholastically.

In summary, the following hypotheses were developed:

1. In learning situations, Jimmy's motivation to learn is weak. He is impulsive and easily distracted.
2. Jimmy's behavior reflects the capacity for reality-appropriate modulations and ego control of his aggression.
3. On occasion, Jimmy's expressions of anger are likely to result in injury to others and a personal loss of self-esteem.
4. Larry's behavior also reflects the capacity for reality-appropriate ego

modulations and control of his aggression.

5. Larry's aggressive expressions tend to boomerang, resulting in self-injury and narcissistic loss.
6. One specific channel for the expression of anger which Larry uses is belittling, derogatory humor.
7. Larry is brighter, more alert, and more inventive than Jimmy.
8. Jimmy's gross motor behavior shows greater strength and coordination than Larry's.
9. The environment contributes to the frustration of Jimmy's attempts to learn.

The hypotheses were evaluated using the 114 remaining stories in the series. That is, stories relevant to each hypothesis were selected and judged as to whether or not their content supported or disagreed with it. They were evaluated in part by comparing Jimmy's and Larry's behaviors. For example, it was hypothesized that in learning situations Jimmy was more easily distracted and that the environment contributed to the frustration of his attempts to learn. Fifteen stories depict situations in which someone is reading, trying to read, or in school. In four of these Jimmy is distracted, Larry is distracted only once. We would say then that Jimmy is more likely than Larry to respond to intruding stimuli. However, there is no significant evidence that the environment itself is more distracting for Jimmy than for Larry. Rather, it appears that in learning situations Jimmy is much more likely to pay attention to extraneous events.

There is good evidence that both boys can consistently subject their aggression to appropriate ego modifications. In twelve stories, Jimmy is seen as appropriately aggressive, and in eighteen stories, Larry assumes this position. Each boy is depicted only once as using poor judgement and letting his aggression get out of control. There is no evidence to support the hypothesis that Jimmy's aggression results in injury to others and loss of self-esteem more frequently than this happens to Larry.

However, there *is* support for the hypothesis that Larry's aggression tends to boomerang. He is likely to take the bull by the horns only to find himself in a dilemma. In looking at the stories which support this idea, it was necessary to consider a significant modification in the hypothesis. Larry "shows off" his skill in riding his bicycle and later in sliding on the ice. In each case he ends up looking rather foolish. In attempting to use a camera he trips and falls, and in driving a "Dodgem car" he loses control. We might say that when the aim of Larry's controlled aggression is narcissistic enhancement, obtained through the admiration of others, he risks a loss of self-esteem. In some cases he gains stature, but more frequently he loses. Jimmy, on the other hand, is less inclined to take such risks, suggesting that either Larry has a greater need for external narcissistic gratification, or that he has a greater capacity to tolerate momentary humiliations and is in a better psychological position to take risks of this sort.

There is also support for the hypothesis that Larry uses humorous derogation of others as a specific outlet for his aggression. The main theme of eight stories includes Larry's belittling others as a significant element. Only once is Jimmy seen laughing at someone else's mistakes or infantile behavior.

There is also support for the idea that Jimmy is stronger and better coordinated than Larry. We see Jimmy hitting a baseball over the trees. He is also slightly bigger than Larry (at least he wears larger snow boots). Probably the best example of how Jimmy is depicted as "the athlete" is in a story about going to the beach. Each child brings a selection of toys to play with. Larry appears with several sand toys. Jimmy arrives carrying a ball and bat.

In light of the fact that the chief purpose of this multiethnic primer was to help nonwhite children learn to read by providing characters with whom they might identify, the hypotheses concerned with Jimmy's tendency to be distracted are of particular interest. Of equal importance, however, is the hypothesis that Larry is more intelligent than Jimmy. The current social emphasis on equal learning opportunities for nonwhite children is based on the proposition that they are as well endowed intellectually as white children, a proposition lacking universal public acceptance. The question here is whether or not this proposition is upheld in these stories.

Finally there is the question of which boy is more intelligent. Larry seems to be the brighter of the two in twenty-four stories, Jimmy in nine stories. Some examples will help to illustrate the ways in which Larry's intelligence is demonstrated. First, in eighteen stories, Larry shows a greater ability to relate elements of the external world to one another in order to arrive at a new solution. In some cases he fools Jimmy and makes him look woefully inept. On a number of occasions he is simply more successful than his playmate. For example, he and

Debbie put on makeup and act in a puppet show, while Jimmy provides musical accompaniment on the harmonica. His finger paintings become the center of attraction, while Jimmy fails to finish his paintings. There are several stories in which Larry's adaptive superiority is clearly demonstrated. In one, David's ball bounces under the lawn sprinkler. Jimmy attempts to retrieve it by putting a box over his head to avoid getting wet. While he is doing this, Larry calmly walks to the faucet and shuts the water off. In another instance, the boys are faced with the problem of getting the dog out of the doghouse. Jimmy impulsively sticks his head into the doghouse and tries to pull the animal out. Larry succeeds where Jimmy failed by enticing the dog out of the house with food. Later, in another story, Jimmy uses some food to entice a monkey down from a tree in a park, demonstrating that at least he can learn from his white peer.

In summarizing these findings we can see distinct character attributes in each of these two boys. Jimmy Black is a child with athletic potentialities who is less motivated to read and learn in school than his peers. He tends to be impulsive rather than inventive, alert, and creative. He is not impulsively aggressive, however, being able to successfully modulate his aggression in age-appropriate ways. Larry is a different kind of boy. Frequently, before he resorts to action, he momentarily stops to think in order to determine the best course of action. He is not noticeably easily distracted, but he *is* alert to elements in reality which he can use creatively to solve a problem. He is willing to risk a momentary loss of self-esteem if there is a chance that he can gain the adulation of others. And yet he is not a constant show-off and is probably not a boy who is dependent upon external narcissistic supplies. Rather, the stories suggest that he is psychologically comfortable with himself and can recover quickly from brief humiliations. Finally, he is socially secure to the extent that he can make fun of others frequently enough so that his belittling, derogatory, fun-poking humor appears as one of his preferred avenues for the expression of aggression.

ANALYSIS OF THE BLACK AND WHITE FATHERS

The two fathers appear in some of the stories, limiting the comparisons that can be made. Mr. Black appears in sixteen stories, Mr.

White in fifteen, and they are seen together in two additional stories. Despite their limited appearance, the stories do show them as having definite individual characteristics.

The two stories in which both appear provide a convenient starting point. In the first, we see the two families discovering each other while watching a parade. Little Suzy White asks her father for a flag. He responds by buying five American flags, one for each of his own and Mr. Black's children. In the other story Mr. Black has been forced to concentrate on the children rather than on his own fishing. Mr. White invites the children to go for a ride in a motorboat, saying, "We will let Jimmy's father get a fish."

In each story Mr. White demonstrates more economic resources than Mr. Black. Other stories support this. He has a nicer car than Mr. Black who says in the last story of the series after looking at automobiles in a used-car lot, "The old brown car is the one for us after all." Mr. Black is seen spending money on only one occasion: he gives his boys some coins so that they can go to the store with Larry White who has arrived with some money. Mr. White spends money in five stories. He also has a Polaroid camera. His son has a bicycle before Jimmy Black does. This difference between the two men is not unlike the real world in which the average income level of black families is lower than that of whites.

What other characteristics are discernible? In an earlier study of these primers (described in Chap. 5), it was found that an inordinately high incidence of masculine activities ended in failure. That is, when the main activity in the story was judged to be masculine, it was more apt to end in a failure to achieve a goal than if the activity was feminine. Thus, the portrayal of masculinity was coupled with the likelihood of failure. This finding is not limited to multiethnic primers (discussed in Chap. 1), but here the incidence of masculine failure was higher than in any other series. Moreover, the authors of this series stated that they thought that the issue of masculinity was of extreme importance. In particular they regarded the presence of the black father as important to the children reading the books.

Some of the initial impressions suggested that it might be fruitful to study the degree to which each of these men was consistently masculine. The closest Mr. White comes to performing a feminine task is in carving a pumpkin with a large knife to make a jack-o'-lantern for his daughter. Mr. Black, on the other hand, is shown performing feminine tasks in seven stories or in nearly half of his appearances. Actually his first appearance in the stories is as a symbolic but not well-disguised mother. He comes home, unzippers his jacket, and out pops a baby kitten! Subsequently he is shown looking for a child's sock, cooking hot dogs, washing dishes, and taking over the housework when his wife is away. Thus, unlike his white neighbor, Mr. Black is a man who is required to assume feminine responsibilities, and, going back to his kitten-bearing entrance, is symbolically less than completely masculine to begin with.

The significant difference between the relative intelligence and creativity shown by Jimmy and Larry suggests a similar comparison between their fathers. Neither father is seen very frequently in situations requiring any noteworthy intelligence, a rather negative comment on the kinds of adult masculine models exhibited in these books. This is the usual state of affairs for any children's primer. Mr. Black demonstrates the capacity to plan and build a cement walk, to rake leaves, and trim the grass. Mr. White can fix a simple toy, carve a pumpkin, and knows enough to go to the dog pound to find a lost dog. When Mr. White's family is caught in the rain, his son is bright enough to point out the park shelter, an observation his father missed in his haste to pack up and go home. Mr. Black looks less than intelligent on one occasion also. He finishes assembling his son's new bike only to discover that he has put the handlebars on backwards. Although neither father is shown to his best advantage, neither is more creative, intelligent, nor adaptive than the other. In summary then, Mr. White is presented as a man with greater economic power than Mr. Black. Mr. White is consistently masculine. Although Mr. Black is strong, sports -minded, and somewhat skillful in using tools, he frequently assumes passive, feminine, maternal, housekeeping roles.

Finally we should return to the two stories in which both men appear, since up to this point a crucial element has been ignored. In both stories Mr. White assists Mr. Black. He helps in the parade story by providing flags for the Black children. Later he takes the children off Mr. Black's hands so that Mr. Black can do some fishing by himself. The significance of these two actions is greater than one might think at first glance for two reasons. In the first place, in no story does Mr. Black have an opportunity to reciprocate even if he desired to do so.

Secondly, Mr. White does not ask Mr. Black if he wants flags for his children or if he wants to fish alone. Evidently Mr. White *assumes* that this is what his neighbor wishes. To make such assumptions suggests the kind of implicit feelings of superiority some members of the majority group hold, consciously or unconsciously, toward minority group members. Mr. White evidently "knows what's good for" Mr. Black.

One could speculate that when faced with these offers of assistance by his neighbor, Mr. Black "goes along" with the idea, but inwardly he is negative about it. It may be that he enjoys fishing with his own and his neighbor's children, that he doesn't like motorboats churning up the water and leaving the fish-killing oils in the water and wants his children to grow up cathecting the pastoral, contemplative values inherent in the use of rod and reel rather than following the current widespread cathexis of speed, power, and the faster and the bigger the better. Or, while watching the parade he may have been about to point out the one black musician in the band (as illustrated), and tell his children that he is the local Uncle Tom. Or, perhaps he was thinking about the social injustices which have occurred under the flag which Mr. White graciously bestowed on his children a moment later. If we could confirm these projective assumptions, we might be moved to suggest to Mr. White that his attitudes are not necessarily conducive to the healthy development of sound relationships between any two adults, never mind individuals from divergent ethnic backgrounds.

However, these speculations arise from the projection of this writer's attitudes into Mr. Black and are not supported by what else we know about him. He is a man who is not consistently masculine, who assumes a passive-feminine position. Given this information, it may well be that he is a man who responds to offers of assistance with expressions of gratitude. Putting together the fact that he is feminine, that he is not portrayed as protesting Mr. White's assumed attitudes of superiority, and that he does not reciprocate with offers of assistance, we are left with the very likely possibility that Mr. Black is an Uncle Tom himself.

The depiction of some aspects of the black characters as reflecting an implied basic inferiority is a value judgment, of course, and requires an explicit evaluation of whether or not the judgment is applicable. For example, one might say that the presentation of Mr. White as possessing greater economic power is to present him as a superior person, since the more money one has, the better he is. Others might argue that this has nothing to do with the dimension since superiority as a person has nothing to do with economics. Besides, since the average income of blacks is lower than that of whites, such a presentation is simply a statement of reality.

Characterizing Mr. Black's mixture of masculine and feminine attributes as "inferior" to Mr. White's consistently masculine behavior requires explanation as well. The realities of employment at this time are such that many black fathers are forced to assume household duties while their wives work. In a sense, then, perhaps such a presentation is, again, more in keeping with reality. Moreover, most fathers are called upon to perform feminine tasks from time to time, and a balance of masculine and feminine orientations can demonstrate a well-developed capacity for ego expression and adaptation.

If we go back to the children for whom these stories were written, however, our perspective changes. From a developmental point of view, sex differentiation remains an essential, primary task for the five- and six-year-old child. In accomplishing the developmental task of establishing his or her own sexual identity, the growing child makes extensive use of identification with adults and older children. Consistent masculinity is of great psychic importance to the first grade boy, and the more masculine behavior he perceives in the adult male, the greater the value of that adult as an identification figure. The male child tends to be threatened by feminine behavior in adult males. In this sense then, Mr. Black has been made less attractive to the black boy striving for first-class citizenship.

To return to the two boys, Larry's greater alertness, creativity, and integrative capacity requires comment in terms of the superiority-inferiority dimension. Here the issue is a highly sensitive one, that of the relative intellectual capacities of blacks and whites. The economic disparity between the two groups can be seen as a consequence of social conditions of long standing. The feminine behavior of Mr. Black may reflect certain current social conditions, and he does show a capacity for masculine behavior equal to that of Mr. White. The issue of intellectual capacity is different, however, because of the connotations of this concept for most psychologists, educators, and the public at large. Whatever the scientific evidence, it is generally accepted that a person's intellectual potential is determined largely by heredity and is relatively immutable. Therefore, we are dealing here with a personal characteristic which is closer to a child's self-concept and is less affected by social conditions at least in the eyes of the child. To present Jimmy as being less intelligent than Larry is to ask black children to incorporate a sense of intellectual inferiority. In addition, while economic and social conditions may change as a consequence of new political directions, many educators doubt that the basic intellectual capacities of members of a group can be so improved. Thus, we might speculate that this kind of incorporation includes with it a sense of hopelessness for the child.

Let us turn to the finding that Jimmy is a boy with a relatively low capacity to sustain his learning activities. This is syntonic with one aspect of popular conceptions and documented observations of culturally disadvantaged children in the classroom, that the children are not motivated. The authors have communicated that Jimmy, a black, brings to the classroom this same attitude toward learning. It would seem that in identifying with Jimmy, the children who read these books may perpetuate and exacerbate a characteristic which will interfere with their educational growth.

Larry's greater proclivity for taking narcissistic risks is more difficult to interpret. When taking this finding together with his frequent use of belittling and fun-poking humor, it suggests that he has a greater freedom of expression than Jimmy, both for narcissistic and aggressive wishes. His freedom to call attention to himself and to humorously belittle others is comparable to the expressive freedom of a comedian who, in order to gain self-esteem, risks failure by ridiculing himself or others.

Who is it that Larry uses for the object of his aggressively loaded humor? There are ten stories in which the main activity ends with Larry laughing at or directing others' laughter toward someone else. Twice he pokes fun at his little sister. In the other eight instances he is deriding a black person. There is an indication then of racial selectivity in Larry's choice of objects for his derisive humor.

This is a troubling suggestion because together with other data it indicates the communication of a prejudicial position. This hypothesis, if sustained, has serious implications, and deserves careful analysis. First, its strength is weakened by the high number of appearances of blacks in the story. Since the black family is the central one, its members appear more frequently, and, therefore, are more available as objects of his humor. On the other hand, there is only one instance in which *this kind* of humor was directed toward a white by a black.

The children in these stories laugh *at* each other on a number of occasions. It is important to clarify two different kinds of situations in which children are laughed at. The humor used by Larry and which is being discussed here consists of laughter at someone who makes a mistake in the process of a rational attempt at problem solving. Larry is laughed *at* on several occasions, but this occurs when he fails in his attempts to show off his fantasied skills. These are occasions in which Larry has deliberately put himself "on stage," so to speak, where he has decided to risk the possibility of a minor humiliation. By reviewing all instances in which one or several characters poked fun at one another, without establishing the statistical significance of the finding, the evidence suggests that Larry is the only one who makes consistent use of belittling others, and in most instances, he directs his humor toward blacks. There certainly is positive evidence that while he pokes fun deliberately at blacks, blacks do not make fun of his mistakes in problem solving.

The comparison of Larry to a comedian comes to mind again. Changes in the public use of ethnic humor have occurred during the last twenty years in this country. Prior to about 1950, it was acceptable (indeed expected) for radio programs, movies, and comedians to engage in the humorous depreciation of blacks. The popularity of minstrel shows, "Step 'n' Fetchit" roles in the movies, and Amos 'n' Andy are examples of this social phenomenon. Since the late 1950's the media has attempted with varying degrees of success, to show greater respect for minority groups. At the same time, the satirical comedian reappeared as a significant entertainment entity. Mort Sahl and others gained respect, fame, and widespread acceptance for their humorous derogations of majority group prejudices, while Amos 'n' Andy disappeared. The numbers and followers of these monologists grew rapidly, followed by the somewhat startling appearance of black comedians, including Dick Gregory, Nipsey Russell, and Godfrey Cambridge, whose jokes about the white community gained an acceptance previously experienced only from black audiences. Flip Wilson, is able, in the same monologue, to make both whites and blacks laugh at his derogations of both white and black stereotyped attributes. Much of Bill Cosby's material evokes memories of childhood which are common to individuals from a number of ethnic backgrounds.

Larry's proclivity and Jimmy's hesitancy to laugh at others' mistakes and shortcomings may be analogous to what was acceptable and expected in the days of Amos 'n' Andy. Perhaps this is attributable to a publication lag. More likely it is a reflection of the persistence of unconscious attitudes toward blacks despite the changes that have occurred in American expressive humor as it appears in the public media. The important point here is that these attitudes influenced the story content in a series of books designed to make life more equitable for black children, written by authors who are dedicated to improving the educational system. It is one more indication of the strength of those aspects of American beliefs which, since the nation's beginning, have made the attainment of our national goals impossible.

REFERENCES

Moynihan, P. *The Negro family: the case for national action*. Washington: U. S. Department of Labor, Office of Planning and Research, 1965.

Whipple. G. *Appraisal of the city schools' reading program*. Detroit: Detroit Public Schools, Division of Improvement of Instruction, Language Education Department, 1963.

CHAPTER 7

HOW DIFFERENT ARE MULTIETHNIC URBAN PRIMERS?

Richard R. Waite

This chapter is concerned only with the environmental, cultural, and outcome ratings in seven multiethnic series. Since in several cases the same or nearly the same authors wrote multiethnic series as wrote traditional series we have the opportunity to make important comparisons which provide data relevant to questions about multiethnic primers.

METHOD

Seven publishers' series, identified in Table 7-1, were subjected to content analyses using the content dimensions and procedures de-

This chapter first appeared, in its original version, as: Waite, R. R. "Further Attempts to Integrate and Urbanize First Grade Reading Textbooks: A Research Study," *Journal of Negro Education*, Winter 1968, 62-69. Reprinted by permission.

scribed in Chapter 1. Agreements among raters for the ratings of the dimension were similar to those previously reported.

Series A, reported in Chapter 5, and Series F and G represent the results of new and innovative efforts by publishers. They are departures from established patterns in the writing of American first grade primers. The other four publishers previously published traditional series widely used by school systems throughout the country. The "national sample," with which the multiethnic series are compared, is a summation of the stories in twelve traditional series. Content analyses of the 1,307 stories of this sample were reported in Chapter 1.

Table 7-1
Identification of Series A-G

Series	Publisher	Series Title	Year
A	Follett	City Schools Reading Program	1965
B	Houghton-Mifflin	Reading for Meaning Series (4th ed.)	1966
C	Scott, Foresman	New Basic Readers Curriculum Foundation Series	1965
D	Harper & Row	Basic Reading Program	1966
E	Macmillan	Macmillan Reading Program	1965
F	Macmillan	Bank Street Readers	1965
G	Chandler	Chandler Language-Experience Readers	1966

The ratings of Environmental Setting, Ethnic Composition, and Outcome of Activity were tabulated. Comparisons between series were made in an effort to determine whether the findings obtained with Series A characterized multiethnic series in general. Comparisons with the national sample also were made. Finally, where the authors of multiethnic series had previously written a traditional series, comparisons between both their efforts were made in terms of the dimensions of interest here.

RESULTS AND DISCUSSION

Table 7-2 shows the Environmental Setting ratings for each multiethnic series and for the national sample. It is apparent that the Surburban setting is the preferred one in Series A through D, with

Series E showing a nearly even number of Suburban and Rural settings. Only Series F and G emphasize Urban settings. Series A, which was intended to be an urban series, is predominantly Suburban, although it is more Urban than B through E. The two innovative series, F and G, have succeeded in their efforts to present stories in Urban settings, and are clearly different from the other series.

Table 7-2

Environmental Setting Ratings
(Number and Percentage of Stories in Each Category)

Series	Urban	Suburban	Rural	Not Clear	Make-Believe	Total
A	22 (19%)	71 (60%)	4 (3%)	10 (8%)	11 (10%)	118
B	3 (2)	87 (65)	34 (26)	9 (7)	0 (0)	133
C	8 (7)	46 (40)	14 (12)	42 (37)	4 (4)	114
D	2 (1)	86 (52)	24 (15)	40 (24)	13 (8)	165
E	2 (2)	47 (38)	50 (41)	23 (18)	1 (1)	123
F	48 (70)	2 (3)	2 (3)	16 (24)	0 (0)	68
G	80 (81)	1 (1)	0 (0)	13 (13)	5 (5)	99
National Sample	18 (2)	499 (38)	254 (19)	469 (36)	67 (6)	1,307

Thus the authors of the major publishing companies' series (B through E) have perpetuated the portrayal of children in a nonurban environment. For the inner-city child, whatever his ethnic background, to read these books is to read about children experiencing conditions quite unlike those with which he is familiar. In this respect, they are even more like the all-white national sample than is Series A. On the other hand, the two innovative series, F and G, represent a clear departure from the major publishers' series and provide the inner-city child with stories about his own immediate world.

Table 7-3 shows the extent to which each multiethnic series contains characters from different ethnic groups. Within each series, stories were classified according to the combinations of ethnic groups represented by the characters. "WAS" signifies that *all* characters in a given story were judged to be of white Anglo-Saxon background. Nothing in the story's content or its pictures indicated that one or more of the characters is of some other racial or national background.

In constructing and labeling the groupings of characters according to ethnic background, the research group experienced an amount of difficulty inordinately greater than the cognitive task at hand. For example, questions arose as to whether they were "cultural" groups or "ethnic" groups. Neither word (according to Webster) is adequate since the distinguishing attribute of one group is racial, another is national background, and others (not included in this study) are religious. The overriding criterion of each group, it should be remembered, is identifiability. Since characters of different backgrounds have been introduced into these stories deliberately by their authors, the reader of the books has little or no difficulty in identifying which groups are involved.

Table 7-3

Ethnic Composition Ratings
(Number and Percentage of Stories in Each Category)

Series	WAS Only	One Non-WAS Group Only	Black and WAS Only	Other Combinations	No Real People
A	7 (6%)	17 (14%)	46 (39%)	35 (30%)	13 (11%)
B	105 (79)	0 (0)	17 (13)	0 (0)	11 (8)
C	56 (49)	16 (14)	30 (26)	5 (4)	7 (7)
D	66 (40)	3 (2)	26 (16)	50 (30)	20 (12)
E	107 (87)	0 (0)	12 (10)	0 (0)	4 (3)
F	3 (4)	3 (4)	47 (70)	8 (12)	7 (10)
G	0 (0)	2 (2)	21 (21)	67 (68)	5 (5)

The use of the label "WAS" may be somewhat misleading. (It is, of course, a form of the semi-popular term WASP, but it proved impossible to identify the characters' religions.) A more accurate description might be Northern European White, which would encompass the many possibilities inherent in the illustrations (Nordic, Celtic, Germanic, Gaelic, Baltic, and even Slavic, to name a few). However, it became apparent that one could get into trouble whichever way one turned, since the abbreviations of Northern European Whites came out NEW, and these characters were anything but new. Rather, they were OLD (Old Line Durables). Finally, the label "WAS" was settled on, since it had existing communication value. Besides, the names of the characters lend credibility to the supposition that they were of Anglo-Saxon heritage. There is an abundance of Dicks, Janes, and Mr. Littles, and an absence of Pierres, Gretchens, and Mr. O'Briens. Never is a Jewish name used.

Of the 1,307 stories in the twelve all-white series (the national sample), only twenty-one include non-WAS characters. In eight of these stories, this occurrence is due to the introduction of an organ-grinder, apparently of Southern European extraction, as judged by the portrayal of the stereotype with curly black hair and mustache. Four others are stories about events in other countries (Spain and India). Two were judged to be non-WAS because of appearance and name. One was called "the Shoeman" and the other "the Appleman," a practice at variance with the use of "Mr. Little," "Mr. Green," etc., in referring to other merchants. Finally, the son of "the Appleman" appears in seven stories and is identified as non-WAS by his curly black hair and his established filial relationship to "the Appleman."

The second classification One Non-WAS Group Only indicates that all the characters in a story were of the same ethnic background and that this background was something other than white Anglo-Saxon. For example, such a story would include only black characters, or only Spanish-American characters, or only characters with Oriental facial features. The Black and WAS stories contain characters judged as white Anglo-Saxon and characters judged as blacks. The fourth grouping, Other Combinations, refers to those stories in which members of different ethnic groups are present, but the combination in something other than blacks and white Anglo-Saxons. Finally, the classification No Real People was used to describe those stories about animals, imaginary humanoids, etc., in which no humans appear.

In looking at Table 7-3, it is obvious that each publishers' series has approached the issue of multiethnicity in its own way. Series A, F, and G contain few stories in which only WAS characters appear. Rather, people from more than one ethnic group are working and playing together in most of the stories. Two of these series, A and F, contain stories in which only blacks and whites appear. Series G features stories in which the characters come from several ethnic groups. Series B, C, D, and E each have a significant number of stories in which only white Anglo-Saxon people are seen. C and D make an attempt to include other ethnic combinations, but B and E pay little more than passing attention (10 to 13 percent of the stories) to the idea of including multiethnic stories in their books. In light of these findings, the two series cannot be legitimately described as multiethnic. This conclusion is reinforced by the ratings in Table 7-2, which indicate that the environmental setting is either Suburban or Rural in 91 percent of the

Series B stories, and 79 percent of the stories in Series E. They simply were not designed for the children from a variety of ethnic backgrounds living in present-day urban cultures.

Table 7-4 lists the frequency distributions of outcome ratings within each series. The results in Series A are those reported earlier. As can be seen, the frequency distribution for Series A is unique; no other series has so few stories in which the main activity ended in Success. Series B and C, however, also differ from the national sample in the same direction. The characters in these stories experience Success in their independent endeavors only about one-half the time or less. Series D through G approximate or exceed the frequency of success experiences in the national sample.

Table 7-4

Outcome Ratings

(Number and Percentage of Stories in Each Category)

Series	Success	Failure	Help	Uncertain
A	26 (22%)	64 (54%)	27 (23%)	1 (1%)
B	55 (41)	54 (41)	17 (13)	7 (5)
C	59 (52)	35 (31)	20 (17)	0 (0)
D	113 (68)	22 (13)	23 (14)	7 (5)
E	75 (61)	24 (19)	18 (15)	6 (5)
F	49 (72)	1 (2)	18 (26)	0 (0)
G	91 (92)	4 (4)	4 (4)	0 (0)
National Sample	832 (64)	340 (26)	120 (9)	15 (1)

An interesting finding which appears in Table 7-4 is the relatively high frequency of Help ratings in the multiethnic series. With the exception of Series G, all of them have more stories in which the goal of the main activity is achieved only because of assistance from someone, usually an adult. The significance of this finding was determined by comparing Series B through G with the national sample. (Series A was omitted because of its obvious uniqueness and the chance that its high frequency of Help ratings would distort the results.) This comparison showed a significant difference in the frequency of Help ratings ($\chi^2 = 11.4$, $p < .001$). Just why multiethnic stories should so frequently include assistance for the characters is difficult to understand. It seems to reflect a kind of subtle bias introduced into the multiethnic series by their authors. Examination of the data indicated that there was no correlation between the outcome ratings and the classification of stories by ethnic grouping. That is, non-WAS children in the stories do not succeed, fail, or need help any more frequently than other children. Nevertheless, the finding is significant, and suggests a poorly understood change in emphasis when authors write multiethnic primers, as will be seen.

The authors of Series B had written an all-white traditional series before they wrote their multiethnic series. We compared these two series, and learned that in addition to the introduction of black characters into 13 percent of the stories, the stories themselves were new and different. The outcome ratings also differed, with the multiethnic series having a lower percentage of Success stories. This difference in outcome ratings was statistically significant ($\chi^2 = 16.3$, $p < .001$).

The only other multiethnic series in which the same authors had written a traditional series was Series D. Here also the stories were new and different, and 60 percent of the stories contained non-WAS characters. Once again, the outcome ratings show significantly lower incidence of Success stories in the multiethnic series ($\chi^2 = 9.5$, $p < .005$).

Series C has a higher frequency of Failure stories than the national sample, but further examination reveals that this finding is not related to the introduction of multiethnic characters. The authors who wrote the stories in that series previously had written a traditional all-white series. The multiethnic series is simply a slight revision of the traditional one, using essentially the same stories but changing the ethnic background of some of the characters in 51 percent of the stories. The ratings of outcome on the two series are identical.

One final aspect of Table 7-4 should be examined. Series G is clearly unlike the other series in terms of the outcome ratings. In 92 percent of its stories, the main activity ends in Success. Eighty-one percent of the stories take place in urban settings. No story contains only white Anglo-Saxon characters. It is without question innovative in other aspects as well (e.g., photographic illustrations, non-WAS teacher, etc.). It is also of interest that it is produced by a company which, as far as can be determined, has not published a traditional series.

Consequently, it is likely that the distribution of Series G is limited compared to series published by larger companies which are well established in the business of producing and selling their reading series to school systems.

In reporting a study such as this one, in which the emphasis is on rating scales, frequency distributions, and statistical comparisons, it is difficult to convey the many attributes of a series which make it unattractive, pallid or unappealing. Suffice it to say that Series G is new and different enough, depicting real children in real situations. After reading a large quantity of pollyannaish stories about essentially the same unreal, smiling children in the same sunshiny, idealized middle-class situations, one finds this series to be attractive, appealing, and stimulating.

CONCLUSIONS

Several conclusions can be drawn from this study. First, what may appear to be a multiethnic first grade reading series may, upon closer inspection, contain few significant characters of ethnic background other than white Anglo-Saxon. Second, the inclusion of "other" ethnic groups in no way implies that the environmental setting of the stories is in any way different from that of the traditional, all-white Suburban-Rural series. Third, multiethnic series are not characterized generally by stories in which the main activity ends in Failure. However, in writing multiethnic series, some authors may have a tendency to emphasize failure and/or need for help more than they do when writing traditional first grade reading books.

CHAPTER 8

MALES AND FEMALES
IN AMERICAN PRIMERS
FROM COLONIAL DAYS
TO THE PRESENT

Sara Goodman Zimet

Both historical and contemporary studies indicate that by the age of six, most children are actively involved in sex role differentiation (Earle, 1899; Kagan, 1964; Oetzel, 1966; Steere, 1964; Sutton-Smith & Rosenberg, 1961). Since we know that boys show uneasiness, anxiety, and anger when they are in danger of behaving in ways regarded as characteristic of the opposite sex, then a clear sex role distinction would appear to be of vital importance to boys. We also know that girls, in addition to seeking out female adult models, are more willing, even eager, to participate with boys in play and in boy-associated activities. Therefore, a strict differentiation in sex role behavior would not be as essential for girls.

The large proportion of activities in the stories in both the standard and multiethnic series judged to be appropriate to both boys and girls

This chapter first appeared, in its original version, as: Zimet, S. G. "Little Boy Lost," *Teachers College Record*, 72: 31-40, 1970. Reprinted by permission.

together, rather than to either boys or girls separately (see Chaps. 1, 5, and 7) along with the growing body of research pointing to the reading difficulties experienced by boys (Money, 1966), suggested an area for further exploration.

In this investigation, therefore, we were interested in finding out if the sex role models portrayed in reading texts used by previous generations of American school children were in accord with the behavior patterns and expectations of the period during which the books were used, and if the male and female sex role models are clearly differentiated during the different historical periods.

METHOD

Selection of Textbooks

Textbooks published prior to the late nineteenth century were limited to those distributed in the northeastern states since books published for the southern and western states varied greatly in content and attitudes presented, depending on regional values. Texts published since the late nineteenth century, however, were written for national distribution and were not specifically written for any one sector of the country. Therefore, no geographic limitation was necessary on the selection of books for this latter time period.

A list of the textbooks in wide use during various periods from 1600 to 1940 was provided by several historians (Carpenter, 1963; Johnson, 1963; Nietz, 1961; Smith, 1965). Final selection was based on their availability to us through interlibrary loans. The choice of modern primers was based on a national survey by Hollins (1955) of the three most frequently used contemporary reading series. Three primary readers representative of each of six historical periods were selected for coding, a total of eighteen readers in all.

All the stories were coded with the exception of two of the three books from the period 1776-1835. These two were compilations of the same compiler. They contained lengthy speeches and dialogues dealing with moral issues. In one book the dialogues were selected for examination here, in the other book ten speeches were chosen at random.

Designation of Appropriate Time Periods

Sex role behavior expectancies were described within the context of the following time periods: Period I, 1600-1776; Period II, 1776-1835; Period III, 1835-1898; Period IV, 1898-1921; Period V, 1921-1940; and Period VI, 1940-1966. These periods as well as the criterion lists were established after a careful examination of the literature from (1) social histories and historical studies of family life (Aries, 1962; Brown, 1958; Calhoun, 1919; Elder, 1899; Gesell, 1946; Gesell & Ilg, 1946; Mead, 1949; Oetzel, 1966; Scudder, 1876; Spencer, 1923; van den Berg, 1961; Woodward, 1946); (2) studies of children's behavior and activity preferences (Croswell, 1898-1899; Newell, 1883; Sutton-Smith & Rosenberg, 1961); and (3) studies analyzing child-rearing manuals and juvenile literature (Kiefer, 1948; Riley, 1963; Ryerson, 1960; Steere, 1964). Most of the data reviewed were rich in descriptive content of the life and times of each of the periods covered in this study.

The significant changes in the behavior expectancies for adults and children over the past 350 years were identified. Both predominant behavior standards and trends toward changes in these standards were noted. Time boundaries were drawn to include trends away from a previous behavior standard, the predominant behavior standard, and trends toward a new standard of behavior.

Although these periods were arrived at empirically, similar time divisions have been used by historians of various aspects of American life (Butts & Cremin, 1953; Calhoun, 1919; Parrington, 1930; Smith, 1965), and give support to the time designations employed by this investigator. The major differences in time designations are found during the period 1776-1860. This span is usually covered as a single unit. To meet the purpose of this study, the recognition of childhood as a special period of life and the introduction of economic and social changes which effected the status and role of women caused this investigator to extend this period to 1898 and to divide it into two separate units, 1776-1835 and 1835-1898.

The Criterion Behavior Lists

The age and sex role behavior expectancies for each of the six time periods were identified to include a list of (1) play activities participated in by boys, girls, and by both boys and girls; (2) behavior expectancy according to age (under and over five years) for boys, girls, and both boys and girls; (3) behavior expectancy for adults (men and women); and (4) a summary statement on children's behavior expectancy. By comparing the age and sex role behavior of the characters in the stories with the age and sex role behavior criterion lists, it was possible to answer, in part, the questions of primary concern to this investigation.

The Coding Units

The same coding manual described in Chapter 1 was used, but the following categories were added which were specifically aimed at assessing sex role behavior: Adult Roles, Dependent and Aggressive Behavior, Behavior Expectancy, Occupations, Illustrations, and Appropriateness Ratings for Time Period, Sex, and Age.

Training the Raters

A male and female graduate student rated the stories with independent agreements between raters calculated to be at a mean of 95 percent over all the categories. The raters divided the books between them and proceeded to code them independently.

Tabulation and Treatment of the Data

Frequency distributions and percentages were tabulated for each of the dimensions described in the coding manual and tables were drawn describing these data. Thus, these data provide a statistical description of the sex role models portrayed in primary reading textbooks used by most American children between the years 1600 and 1966.

RESULTS AND DISCUSSION

A diffuse sex role model was presented in varying and increasing degrees from colonial days to the present. The lack of specificity in sex role was consistent with the diffuse model described in the behavior criterion lists for each of the six periods. To this extent, the models presented were in accord with the times. However, it should be noted that a sex-differentiated model was also described on this list but the portrayal of adult males and females performing similar roles and of boys and girls playing at the same activities was the model selected for presentation in these textbooks. This lack of sex specificity also presented a model of behavior more appropriate to children under five years of age than to children over five years, for whom they were designed. By presenting less mature models of behavior we have ignored the tendency of older children to derogate behavior which was appropriate the year before. A prime insult to a child is to be accused of acting like a baby.

In addition to the consistent pattern of sex role diffusion which shows up from 1600 to the present, another consistent and complimentary pattern appears to evolve. From a character count, it was noted that textbook authors began to increase the number of female characters in the stories as formal education was opened to girls (between 1776 and 1835). This trend continued so that by 1898 and up through 1966, girl characters actually outnumbered boy characters in the texts. Despite the greater frequency of females in the stories, a distinct female behavior identity was avoided.

A possible explanation for the minimizing of sex differences may be found in the desire to present materials that would be acceptable to a classroom grouping of both boys and girls. It remains a curious matter, however, that other alternatives were not attempted. Thus, one might also speculate that the neutral, non-sex-linked male and female behavior described in the stories was an unconscious effort to deny the existence of sexuality in children.

Another developmentally inappropriate model, that of dependency, was consistently sustained throughout the six periods. This behavior was particularly frequent in the books coded from 1921 through 1966, and was rewarded overwhelmingly for both sexes and for all age levels. Here again we have an example of a regressive pull in the presentation of a model of behavior which is more appropriate to children younger than the beginning reader. Since dependency is characteristically associated with females, a feminizing quality also was present in the positive characterization of the male dependent model.

Since it is primarily from adult models that sex role behavior is learned, it was important to examine the characterizations of adults in these primers within the family structure described in the behavior criterion lists. In Periods I and II (1600-1835), the American family was essentially a productive, functional unit. As soon as the young were able to cope with the physical demands of a job, they carried out the same tasks as the adults. Boys emulated their fathers and girls their mothers, and they were treated as adults. In the textbooks coded for these two periods, adult characters predominated. They were portrayed as idealized models of religious and ethical behavior but they were not participating in distinctly male or female roles.

As the productivity function was removed from the home, children no longer had visible work models to emulate and childhood came to be regarded as a period of carefree play. This more affluent America discovered childhood and with the discovery came the separation of children from the adult world. In the books representative of Periods III and IV (1835-1921), adult characters practically disappeared from the texts and were replaced by children and animals. When adults were present, they served as backdrops to the actions going on among the children. Their very absence suggested that the interests and activities of children were different from those of adults despite the fact that these differences were neither spelled out nor made clearly visible. Thus these books carried no specific description of male or female adult roles.

Male and female adult characters entered the books again in sizeable numbers during the last two periods (1921-1966). During that time, they were presented as facilitators of their children's wishes, interests, and needs but without distinct interests and needs of their own. This characterization was consistent with the child-rearing values of family togetherness espoused during these periods. Nevertheless, clearly defined adult male and female behavior was avoided in this portrayal of a child-centered adult model. There also was no reference to the world outside this closely-knit nuclear family.

Thus, from this overall review of the presentation of the adult models in all the books coded for all the six periods, it can be seen that a very limited and restricted prototype of sex role behavior has been portrayed. To this extent, the primary reading texts fell far short of fulfilling their role as an acculturation medium.

By comparing the Adult Roles, Illustrations, and Behavior Messages to the Behavior Criterion Lists for each period, and by reviewing the Environmental Settings of the stories coded in all six periods, it was quite apparent that only one socioeconomic and cultural group was represented in the total sample of texts examined and thus only one possible social class model of sex role behavior was presented.

Perhaps in this sense, what was left out of the content of these primary reading texts is as important as what was put in. The exclusion of the plurality of sex role models that exists in American society suggests that these texts ignored the differences in cultural backgrounds and socioeconomic conditions that account for these differences. It is interesting to speculate whether this was an attempt to unify a diverse people under the white Anglo-Saxon middle-class model in the spirit of egalitarianism, or if this was a reflection of the attitude toward the role of education as a selector and sustainer of tradition. The avoidance of socioeconomic and cultural differences is similar in a sense to the avoidance of sex differences. We are saying, in essence, that by ignoring them or diffusing them we are doing away with the evils and inequities associated with them. This is the old story of treating the symptom rather than the cause. The extent to which sex labels, cultural labels, and socioeconomic labels produce inequities in our society, the inequities should be eliminated, not the differences.

REFERENCES

Aries, P. *Centuries of childhood*. New York: Knopf, 1962.

Brown, D. G. "Sex role development in a changing culture." *Psychological Bulletin*, 1958, *55*, 232-242.

Butts, R. F., & Cremin, L. A. *A history of education in American culture*. New York: Holt, Rinehart & Winston, 1953.

Calhoun, A. A. *A social history of the American family, 1607-1919*, 3 vols. New York: Barnes & Noble, 1919.

Carpenter, C. *History of American schoolbooks*. Philadelphia: University of Pennsylvania Press, 1963.

Child, I. L., Potter, E. H., & Levine, E. M. "Children's textbooks and personality development: an exploration in the social psychology of education." *Psychological Monographs*, 1946, *60*, 1-54.

Clyse, J. "What do basic readers teach about jobs." *Elementary School Journal*, 1959, *59*, 456-460.

Croswell, T. R. "Amusements of Worcester school children." *The Pedagogical Seminary*, 1898-1899, *6*, 314-371.

Earle, A. M. *Child life in colonial days*. New York: Macmillan, 1899,

Elder, R. A. "Traditional and developmental conceptions of fatherhood." *Marriage and Family Living*, 1949, *11*, 98-106.

Gesell, A. L. (ed.). *The first five years of life*. New York: Harper, 1946.

Gesell, A. L., & Ilg, F. *The child from five to ten*. New York: Harper, 1946.

Hollins, W. H. "A national survey of commonly used first grade readers." Unpublished data, Alabama A & M College, 1955.

Holmes, M. B. "A cross-cultural study of the relationship between values and modal conscience." In W. Muensterberger & S. Axelrad (eds.), *The psychoanalytic study of society*. Vol. 1. New York: International Universities Press, 1960, pp. 98-181.

Johnson, C. *Old-time schools and schoolbooks*. New York: Dover Publications, 1963.

Kagan, J. "Acquisition and significance of sex-typing and sex role identity." In M. L. Hoffman & L. W. Hoffman (eds.), *Review of child development research*. Vol. 1. New York: Russell Sage Foundation, 1964, pp. 137-166.

Kiefer, M. *American children through their books, 1700-1835*. Philadelphia: University of Pennsylvania Press, 1948.

Mead, M. *Male and female*. New York: Morrow, 1949.

Money, J. "On learning and not learning to read." In J. Money (ed.), *The disabled reader*. Baltimore: Johns Hopkins Press, 1966, pp. 21-40.

Newell, W. W. *Games and songs of American children*. New York: Harper, 1883.

Nietz, J. A. *Old textbooks*. Pittsburgh: University of Pittsburgh Press, 1961.

Oetzel, R. "Annotated bibliography." In E. E. Maccoby (ed.), *The development of sex differences*. Stanford, Cal.: Stanford University Press, 1966, pp. 223-351.

Parrington, L. V. *Main currents of American thought*. New York: Harcourt, Brace, and World, 1930.

Riley, C. D. "Perceptions concerning children as revealed through poetry for children, 1833-1850, 1875-1890." Unpublished doctoral dissertation, Florida State University, Tallahassee, Fla., 1963.

Ryerson, A. "Medical advice on child rearing, 1550-1900." Unpublished doctoral dissertation, Harvard University, Cambridge, Mass., 1960.

Scudder, H. E. (ed.), *Men and manners in America one hundred years ago*. New York: Scribner, Armstrong, 1876.

Smith, N. B. *American reading instruction*. Newark, Del.: International Reading Association, 1965.

Spencer, A. G. *The family and its members*. Philadelphia: Lippincott, 1923.

Steere, G. H. "Changing values in child socialization: a study of U. S. child rearing literature, 1865-1929." Unpublished doctoral dissertation, University of Pennsylvania, Philadelphia, 1964.

Sutton-Smith, B., & Rosenberg, B. G. "Sixty years of historical change in the game preferences of American children." *Journal of American Folklore*, 1961, *74*, 17-46.

Tennyson, W. W., & Monnens, L. P. "The world of work through elementary readers." *Vocational Guidance Quarterly*, Winter 1963-1964, 85-88.

van den Berg, J. H. *The changing nature of man*. New York: Norton, 1961.

Woodward, W. E. *The way our people lived*. New York: Dutton, 1946.

CHAPTER 9

VALUES AND ATTITUDES IN AMERICAN PRIMERS FROM COLONIAL DAYS TO THE PRESENT

Sara Goodman Zimet

This chapter is concerned specifically with describing the relationship between textbook content and the social values and attitudes held by the "establishment" from colonial days to the present.

THE COLONIAL PERIOD

The readers used by the colonists prior to the Revolution have been described extensively by several historians (Carpenter, 1963; Johnson, 1963; Nietz, 1961). The description of their content bears out the fact that for the early settlers, religion was the overriding characteristic of their lives. In an analysis of the content of these early books, 92 percent was found to be of a religious nature (Nietz, 1961).

This chapter first appeared, in its original version, as: Zimet, S. G. "American Elementary Reading Textbooks: A Sociological Review," *Teachers College Record*, 70: 331-340, 1969. Reprinted by permission.

Interspersed generously with the alphabet and syllabarium were benedictions, catechisms, proverbs, and fables which illustrate well the attitudes, values, and behavior of the colonists. They considered their own values the only correct ones to live by. *The Protestant Tutor* * with its anti-Catholic doctrine, serves as a fine example of the biased content that was purposely introduced to misrepresent and adversely criticize those attitudes, beliefs, or customs not held by the establishment.

The spirit of child-rearing practices in this period is well illustrated in the *New England Primer*,† from the following statements taken from the section entitled, "Lessons from Youth":

FOOLISHNESS is bound up in the Heart of a Child, but Rod of correction shall drive it from him.

LIARS shall have their Part in the Lake which burns with Fire and Brimstone.

UPON the Wicked God shall rain an Horrible Tempest.

This single-minded emphasis on conformity to a Spartan religious life makes one wonder whether indeed they had been successful in achieving this end.

Loyalty to the reigning English monarch was also discernible from the pictures on the frontispiece of the books as well as from the occasional references made in the texts. However, following the Revolution, the king's picture was replaced by a portrait of George Washington and the references made to monarchs were less than edifying.

THE PERIOD OF NATIONAL EXPANSION

The readers in post revolutionary America had a new function to perform, that of developing loyalty to the new nation. Much of the content also reflected the emphasis on developing an intelligent citizenry capable of efficiently discharging their duties. Nationalism, to a large extent, became equated with morality. This created a secular

The Protestant Tutor was the first English textbook printed in America. It had a sizeable circulation judging from the number of editions printed.

†*The New England Primer*, also published under the titles of the *New York Primer* and the *Columbian Primer*, enjoyed an estimated sale of around three million copies.

philosophy which demanded the same kind of rigid conformity that prevailed under the religious doctrine. The religious content in the readers was reduced by 22 percent while content devoted to inculcating morals increased by 25 percent (Nietz, 1961). Thus, the trend at the turn of the eighteenth century was away from a Protestant ethic toward a social ethic (de Charms & Moeller, 1962).

Noah Webster's *Old Blueback** epitomized the new breed of readers. It combined a speller with a reader and included poetry for recitation, speeches of the patriotic leaders of the Revolution and a moral catechism. In addition, it was the first text to attempt to overcome the diversity of dialects, the variety in word structure and the chaos in spelling that existed throughout the colonies.

The nature of the child, his inclinations, tastes, and desires became more and more dominant factors in the choice and arrangement of the subject matter. Illustrations were introduced to make the lessons "a pleasure rather than a task."[†] In 1820 one of the earliest educational toys, a revolving alphabet, was introduced. This indicated a significant shift away from the severe punitive attitude which existed during the colonial period.

The question of literacy for girls was undergoing a change as well. In an early edition of his reader[‡], Caleb Bingham stated that it was hardly worthwhile teaching girls much except sewing and housework. However, in a later edition of another reader[¶], he stated that care in the selection of content suitable for the fairer sex should be given due consideration.

Stories designed specifically to build character through the development of proper moral attitudes and behavior presented a sharp contrast between right and wrong. Evil suffered prompt, severe punishment, and good was as promptly and decisively rewarded. Reforms were astonishingly sudden, successful, and permanent. A prime example of the

---

*The title, *Old Blueback*, was an affectionate reference used in place of the long scholarly title: *A Grammatical Institute of the English Language Comprising an Easy Concise and Systematic Method of Education, Designed for the Use of English Schools in America, Part I Containing a New and Accurate Standard of Pronunciation*.

† Attitudes expressed in Noah Webster, *The Little Reader's Assistant,* 1790, and in H. Mann, *The Columbian Primer,* 1802.

‡ Caleb Bingham, *The Child's Companion,* 178?.

¶ Caleb Bingham, *The American Preceptor,* 1794.

schoolbooks that presented this kind of content were the *McGuffey Readers*, which first appeared between 1836 and 1844 and continued in use until 1920. The dominant value stressed was that of individual salvation through hard work, thrift, and competition, which was quite consistent with the economic individualism of laissez-faire capitalism. It also reflected the high achievement drive created by the technological and industrial revolution that transformed America from a rural agrarian society to an industrialized urban culture.

THE EMERGENCE OF A TECHNOLOGICAL AMERICA

The behavior expected of children continued to be clearly and unequivocally stated in these readers. Throughout the stories, one gets the impression that the world is indeed a serious place, fraught with many problems and tribulations. Learning to live properly in society is a job that requires constant vigilance and concentrated effort. The sources of these difficulties are both external and internal; therefore the child must develop inner powers to protect himself against these evils. In order to accomplish this, the child must follow a clearly stated code of Christian virtues preached daily through the strong authority of the father, who represents unshakeable wisdom and goodness. Hence, social behavior is handed down from an indisputable source through a set of established rules which the child must live up to (Mandel, 1964). The stories are essentially means-oriented rather than goal-oriented so that the achievement sequence more often dwells on obstacles to success and specific means of overcoming them rather than on the goals themselves (McClelland, 1961).

The Rollo series which was published between 1844 and 1860 provides an excellent example of how this cultural pattern is communicated. Although Rollo is a good boy, most of his experiences are unpleasant and have direct consequences. The problem lies in the fact that Rollo is basically filled with bad impulses that must constantly be suppressed.

Rollo interrupts his mother at her work, causing her to make a mistake; Rollo leaves something that has been entrusted to him on a rock while he plays, and he loses it; Rollo loses interest in a tedious job his father gave him to do and he does not get it done on time. Rollo's father is the most important character in the books and in Rollo's life. He presents the goals to be sought and achieved and explains, in detail, why an action is right or wrong. He punishes and rewards; corrects and encourages (Mandel, 1964). As pictured in the stories, Rollo's family life is typical of the child-rearing practices during this time of high achievement motivation. This is indicated by early parental stress on independence training and mastery (de Charms & Moeller, 1962). Hard work is highly honored and rewarded while play is strongly discouraged and judged harshly if combined with work:

> Work while you work,
> Play while you play;
> One thing each time,
> That is the way.
> All that you do,
> Do with your might;
> Things done by halves
> Are not done right
>
> *(McGuffey's Eclectic Primer,* p. 53).

Where literary and historical selections had previously been included for practice in elocution, they now took on a new set of purposes: (1) to replace moralistic fables and stories in the development of good character; and (2) to develop a permanent interest and appreciation in literature (Smith, 1965). Arnold and Gilbert's *Stepping Stones to Literature* and Judson and Bender's *Graded Literature Series* were among the first to introduce folk tales and rhymes into primary readers and to express a conscious concern in their selections for children's interests and levels of maturity.

Since large numbers of children reaching the upper grades could not read, a dissatisfaction with the word method stimulated the desire for developing a new technique for teaching reading. Therefore, the alphabet and spelling word approach was abandoned and replaced (around 1889) with an elaborate phonetic system, using diacritical markings. Also, in an effort to develop comprehension skills, the sentence and story method was introduced (Cutts, 1964). An example from Ward's *Third Grade Reader* illustrated how the new method and content were combined:

George's mother, knowing they had come from the fields, began to ask about the horses . . .

Then George said, "The sorrel is dead, madam; I killed him."

His mother looked grieved. . . .

When he had finished she said gently, "I regret the loss of my sorrel, but I rejoice in my son, who always speaks the truth." (Smith, 1965, p. 137).

As an outgrowth of the aim to develop interest in literature, supplementary reading materials became popular and included additional sets of readers other than the basic text, fairy tales, folklore, and the literary classics.

The advent of professional books and separate courses of study dealing with reading instruction signified the trend toward a scientific consideration of educational content and pedagogy. Edmund Burke Huey's famous study on *The Psychology and Pedagogy of Reading* (1908) is the first book to treat reading instruction scientifically. The emergence of the reading specialist signified the professionalization of this area of education, and more and more attention was given to a careful consideration of reading instruction. Thorndike, Huey, and Parker gave this movement a vigorous push forward which eventuated in dramatic changes in teaching practices.

Through extensive testing programs it was again discovered that few children could read and that those who could read, understood little of what they were reading. This time blame was placed on the meaningless phonetic symbols and the overemphasis on oral reading. Thus, the proponents of silent reading instruction came to the fore. This point of view is well summed up in the following statement:

The social needs of former days required the teaching of expressive oral reading; the social needs of the present require the teaching of effective rapid silent reading: (1) Reading material is abundant; (2) Reading is universal; only a few are unable to read; (3) Communication is very rapid; (4) Written language is the chief means of communication (Smith, 1965, p. 164).

So, as we enter the 1920's, we find an almost complete abandonment of oral reading and phonetics and a strong new emphasis on silent reading for meaning and as a utilitarian asset.

The content of these new readers was made up largely of factual and informational material closely approximating the experiences frequently encountered in the child's daily life. But the long dependence upon folk tales and fables as a means of motivating the interest of young children caused the authors to be afraid to trust a straightforward presentation of this factual material. To cope with this problem, inanimate objects were endowed with life and linguistic ability, and fairies and other imaginary beings were used as media for transmitting the information. Colored illustrations were most common, amounting to as much as 30 percent of the text in the primary readers, indicating, incidentally, quite a refinement of the printing process.

Scientific studies on reading continued to be produced. By 1925 there was an accumulation of studies pointing out the diversity of purposes for reading and the different abilities necessary to achieve them. The findings called attention to the need for a more liberal provision of varied materials and for different methods of instruction to develop these diverse reading habits and abilities. Although this produced a significant increase in the publication of courses of study and teacher's manuals, the instructions they contained were much less dogmatic than the instructions of the past. Teachers were given choices among a wide range of supplementary materials and were encouraged to use their own initiative and originality.

In addition to providing a broad variety of stories, the new readers presented several innovations in an effort to make reading more effective and more meaningful to the child: (1) A scientific approach to readability and vocabulary control was applied. The result, after 1928, was that the vocabulary in the readers had decreased by one quarter. (2) Preprimers were introduced. (3) Words were more frequently repeated in nearly all the primers and first readers, and sometimes in second and third readers as well. (4) Supplementary work pads, charts, and flash cards were used to reinforce the learning of reading words by various kinds of exposure. (5) The systematic study of the basal readers became an established activity. (6) Ability grouping, diagnostic testing, and remedial work were started. (7) The format of the readers reached an all time high of excellence in overall eye appeal. Bright colored pictures made up approximately 40 percent of the content. Print was large and clear and wide margins were allowed on each page.

CONTEMPORARY AMERICA

The reading content of first readers has remained fairly stable. The criticism of the 1940's and 1950's was largely directed at the methods of instruction rather than at the subject matter. During the last ten years, attention has been focused on the kinds of messages that are being communicated through the content, and on the adverse effects these messages have on a significant proportion of our population. The critics relate the character of these reading texts to a very fundamental change in the American culture itself.

The technological and economic advances of the nineteenth and twentieth centuries and the aftermath of the two world wars inevitably exerted an influence on the ways in which the individual viewed other people and the world at large. Increases in population and urbanization, expanding literacy, and the intensive development of mass media, all helped spur the move away from the "inner-directedness" of, for example, Rollo to the "other-directedness" of contemporary readers. The dominant values of individual salvation through hard work, thrift, and competition were gradually replaced by a belief in togetherness, generosity, and gregariousness as the ultimate needs of the individual. Therefore, a significant shift occurred from a dependence on personal-institutional relationships to a dependence upon interpersonal relationships (McClelland, 1961).

Contemporary America, as seen through these readers, is an other-directed society in which the individual is not motivated to act by traditional institutional pressures but by pressures from others whose requests or demands are respected enough to produce compliance (McClelland, 1961). Individuals enter into relationships for specific reasons, and these relationships are generally controlled by the opinions and wishes of others. A look at the world of Dick and Jane (of the 1950 Scott, Foresman series) discloses a dramatic depiction of this "new" America.

Dick and Jane's world is a friendly one, populated by good, smiling people who are ready and eager to help children whenever necessary. Strangers, therefore, are not to be mistrusted but viewed as potential helpmates. Human nature and physical nature are also cooperative and friendly rather than competitive and conspiring. There are no evil impulses to be controlled. Instead, free rein and encouragement is given for seeking more and more fun and play. Life in general is easy and comfortable; frustrations are rare and usually overcome quite easily. Combining work with play, seeking out new friends, and giving generously are all amply rewarded by nature, adults, and one's peers. There is an apparent lack of negative example in these stories, so that a code of ethics is not included in the content. Yet the stories seem to illustrate, without overt preaching, the virtues of honesty, fair play, cooperation, family solidarity, friendship, cleanliness, and forgiveness (Klineberg, 1963). Furthermore, one does not find the child's base of authority in traditional sources. The text is almost exclusively conversation among children; there is very little interaction with parents. It would appear, then, that the child's identity is confirmed and that his social behavior is molded by his peer group (Mandel, 1964).

However, the Dick and Jane type of text displays a marked ethnocentrism and socioeconomic-centrism:

One might conclude from these books that Americans are almost exclusively Caucasian, North European in origin and appearance, and are quite well-to-do. Poverty does exist but only in stories set in a foreign environment or in fairy tales. Foreign nationalities as well as American minority groups are placed in either an unfavorable light or are treated inadequately. Religion is rarely mentioned, but Christian religious observance is over-emphasized with no hint of the range or variety of observances found among different religious groups (Klineberg, 1963, p. 75).

In reality, however, America is a pluralistic society, a society of diversity and complex problems and, in fact, "life [in America] is not always a sun-drenched Sunday afternoon" (Jennings, 1964). Despite the fact that 60 percent of Americans live in cities, city life is largely ignored in these readers. In line with this, research studies have pointed out that the cultural inappropriateness of the stories has been an important contributing factor to the low reading achievement of culturally different youth (Whipple, 1964). Very recently this has stimulated several textbook publishers to produce readers which take cultural differences into account. These readers are designed for children from all economic, social, and cutural backgrounds and are aimed at further democratizing American reading texts (see Chaps. 6, 7, and 8). Dr. John Niemeyer, president of Bank Street College, has pointed out that the city child's world is not the only one neglected in traditional readers: "Kids from large families, or one-parent homes, children who wear glasses, youngsters who are short, tall, slim or stocky—they all belong in any but a falsely glamorized fantasy world" (Michalak, 1965).

With the increased exposure of children at all ages to the mass media, their interests have broadened and changed. The readers, although professing to reflect these interests, have not kept up with the changing times (Zimet, 1966). The very fact that a higher incidence of reading retardation is found among boys has also led to the assumption that there is a sex inappropriateness in the kinds of activities depicted in the stories. And if all this is not bad enough, it is also felt that unnecessary barriers to the intellectual development of children are perpetuated by the adherence to outdated vocabulary lists and readability formulas, as well as to the proliferation of anthropomorphism and animism in the content of the readers (Klineberg, 1963).

Striking differences exist between some aspects of reading textbooks of the early colonial period and the contemporary world of Dick and Jane. Changes in the content over the years have reflected society's concern for increasing the literacy of the population as well as for communicating its cultural values. As our scientific knowledge of the child in a dynamically changing society has increased, the more subtle factors influencing children's attitudes have been recognized. Therefore, if we are to accomplish our goals of literacy and transmission of appropriate cultural patterns more effectively, a conscious application of research findings to textbook writing is essential.

REFERENCES

Carpenter, C. *History of American schoolbooks*. Philadelphia: University of Pennsylvania Press, 1963.

Cutts, W. *Teaching young children to read*. Bulletin No. 19. Washington: Office of Education, U. S. Department of Health, Education and Welfare, 1964.

de Charms, R., & Moeller, G. "Values expressed in American children's readers." *Journal of Abnormal and Social Psychology*, 1962, *64*, 136-142.

Henry, J. "Reading for what?" Claremont Reading Conference, Twenty-Fifth Yearbook. Claremont Cal.: Claremont Graduate School Curriculum Laboratory, 1961, pp. 19-35.

Jennings, F. "Textbooks and trapped idealists." *Saturday Review*, January 18, 1964, pp. 57-59, 77-78.

Johnson, C. *Old-time schools and schoolbooks*. New York: Dover, 1963.

Klineberg, O. "Life is fun in a smiling, fair-skinned world." *Saturday Review*, February 16, 1963, pp. 75-77, 87.

Mandel, R. L. "Children's books: mirrors of social development." *Elementary School Journal*, 1964, *64*, 190-199.

McClelland, D. C. *The achieving society*. Princeton, N. J.: Van Nostrand, 1961.

McGuffey's eclectic primer. New York: American Book, 1909.

Michalak, J. "City life in primers." *The Herald Tribune*, January 26, 1965.

Nietz, J. A. *Old textbooks*. Pittsburgh: University of Pittsburgh Press, 1961.

Smith, N. B. *American reading instruction*. Newark, Del.: International Reading Association, 1965.

Whipple, G. "Multicultural primers for today's children." *Education Digest*, 1964, *29*, 26-29.

Zimet, S. G. "Children's interests and story preferences: a critical review of the literature." *Elementary School Journal*, 1966, *67*, 366-374.

CHAPTER 10

ATTITUDES AND VALUES IN PRIMERS FROM THE UNITED STATES AND TWELVE OTHER COUNTRIES

Sara G. Zimet, J. Lawrence Wiberg, & Gaston E. Blom

While studying the motivational content of primary reading textbooks in the United States, the presence of certain attitudes and values in the story content impressed the investigators. Such attitudes recurred with sufficient frequency and consistency that it seemed possible to establish an attitude profile characterizing them. "Attitude" was defined as an attribute or characteristic, either personal or impersonal, to which a value, such as good-bad, superior-inferior, desirable-undesirable, useful-not useful, wanted-unwanted, important-unimportant, could be affixed. Other investigators (Child, Porter, & Levine, 1946; Holmes, 1960; McClelland, 1961) gave evidence that elementary reading textbooks seemed to reflect national characteristics, modalities, attitudes and values. The question was raised if primers

This chapter first appeared, in its original version, as: Zimet, S. G., Wiberg, J. L., and Blom, G. E. "Attitudes and Values in Primers from the United States and Twelve Other Countries," *Journal of Social Psychology*, 84: 167-174, 1971. Reprinted by permission.

from the United States and other countries presented attitude profiles characteristic of a given country which would be measurably different in a cross-national comparison.

The purpose of this chapter is to present a method of cross-national study of the content of first grade reading textbooks, to indicate that attitudes are presented in textbooks and represent a means of socialization, to demonstrate that cross-national differences and similarities can be determined, and to present some of the results in descriptive terms.

METHOD

A long checklist of attitudes and values and their corresponding synonyms was obtained (Henry, 1960). Attitude scales were constructed from this checklist. The scales and a manual for instruction in its use were devised to systematically code and characterize the attitude content of primer stories. Scales that seemed, from pilot studies, to be too ambiguous, too general, or too rare to measure attitudes were eliminated. The attitude scales that appeared to measure the same dimension were clustered together. As the scales were applied to new countries, some additional attitude scales were constructed. For example, primer series from West Germany dealt with children placing flowers on a grave and playing in the cemetery. This and other stories prompted the addition of the attitude cluster, "recognition or portrayal of death, infirmity, illness and danger." Thus, an attitude scale represented an attitude behavior that could be defined and for which illustrations could be given, and on which at least 75 percent agreement between raters could be obtained. A final total of 40 attitude scales resulted.

The attitude scales were then arranged into three groups: Cultural Posture, Other-Directed Posture, and Inner-Directed Posture (see

Table 10-1). Cultural Posture scales captured how people live in terms of what environmental settings are presented, what a country is like, and what collective symbols are stressed. Other-Directed Posture scales represented specific interactional behavior between characters or groups of characters. Inner-Directed Posture scales contained attitudes that motivated or guided the behavior of an individual character or homogeneous set of characters.

Textbooks used in this study consisted of beginning reading texts from the United States and twelve foreign countries: England, France, India, Israel, Italy, Japan, Mexico, Norway, Russia, South Korea, Turkey, and West Germany. Illustrations and translated word content were used as a basis for the ratings. It was recognized that there was a disadvantage in using translated material and in employing scales based on English word usage with an American cultural frame of reference. This has probably introduced an American-English cultural bias into the findings. It would have been preferable to have had the scales defined in the native language and the primers coded from the original material by raters from that country.

The experimental units of this study were the individual stories in each book. These were well defined by titles, illustrations, and plots. A total of 60 stories was randomly selected for each country except for South Korea where only 46 stories were available and all were used. Results for South Korea were based on a projected 60 stories.

The process of rating the stories consisted of using two trained raters who first scored the stories independently in batches of twenty at a time. From the very nature of the attitude scales and the material to which they were applied, difficulty was encountered in achieving consistently high interrater reliability. As mentioned earlier, only those scales were used on which at least 75 percent interrater agreement was obtained. However, disagreements in rating the stories were resolved in a group conference with the investigators. Thus, the data which were used for the analyses reported in this paper represent consensus data.

Table 10-1

Attitude Scales

Cultural Posture	Other-Directed Posture	Inner-Directed Posture
1. Oldness, traditionalism, antiquity, ancient times	13. Caring, helping, aiding, assisting, nurturing, protecting	28. Exploring, curiosity, discovering, inquiring
2. Recognition of other countries' nationalities, ethnic groups, and cultures	14. Uncaring, unhelping, neglecting, disregarding	29. Ambition, striving, aspiring, persistence, initiative
3. Family togetherness	15. Selfishness, possessiveness, greediness, not sharing	30. Lassitude, laziness, lack of ambition
4. Reference to economic transaction	16. Conforming, complying, compromising, conceding, acquiescing, consenting	31. Motor competency, motor dexterity, agility
5. War, warfare, militarism, weaponry	17. Nonconforming, uncompromising, unyielding, disagreeing, disputing, being obstinate	32. Motor incompetence, motor ineptness, clumsiness, physical carelessness
6. Peace, pacifism, armistice	18. Independence	33. Intelligence, alertness, cleverness, capability, attentiveness
7. Nationalism, patriotism	19. Role playing, learning (not necessarily classroom), imitation (copying others)	34. Ignorance, inalertness, stupidity, intellectual incompetence

Cultural Posture	Other-Directed Posture	Inner-Directed Posture
8. Religiousness, devotion to God	20. Working, laboring, toiling	35. Cleanliness, orderliness, neatness, tidiness
9. Education in schools	21. Play, sport, recreation, amusement (as an activity not an affect)	36. Dirtiness, disorderliness, sloppiness, untidiness, disorganization
10. Social regulation and structure, social rules and laws	22. Obedience to authority, deference to authority	37. Courage, bravery, daring, boldness, valor, fortitude, fearlessness
11. Recognition or portrayal of death, infirmity, illness, injury or realistic danger	23. Disobedience to authority, defiance of authority	38. Cowardice, lack of courage, "chicken"
12. Presence of food or drink	24. Interactional physical aggressiveness	39. Physical strength, powerfulness, stoutness, brawniness
	25. Interactional passivity	40. Physical weakness, physical impotence, lacking in physical power
	26. Competitiveness, rivalry	
	27. Cruelty, meanness, maliciousness, tormenting (beyond teasing), ruthlessness	

RESULTS AND DISCUSSION

It appears that countries differ in the extent to which they utilize primary reading texts as a means of socialization. This is indicated by the somewhat comprehensive list of attitudes applied. Table 10-2 demonstrates that the frequency of attitudes present in the 60-story samples varies considerably from country to country. South Korea and India together have over twice as many ratings as do France, Israel, and Turkey combined.

Table 10-2
**Total Number of Attitudes Present in the
60-Story Sample of Each Country**

Country	Rank	Number of Attitudes
South Korea	1	456
India	2	433
England	3	316
Mexico	4	310
Japan	5	295
Norway	6	290
Russia	7	281
United States	8	271
West Germany	9	269
Italy	10	267
Israel	11	251
Turkey	12	251
France	13	248

When the specific attitudes are looked at as to their frequency of occurrence in the total sample of 780 stories, several patterns emerge. Caring and Nurturing (F=428), Playing (F=347), Presence of Food or Drink (F=318) and Working (F=303), are the four most frequently rated attitudes in the 780 stories (see Table 10-3). All but the Presence of Food or Drink are in the Other-Directed group. None of the four fall into the Inner-Directed group. This would seem to suggest that there is a more persistent attempt to foster an other-directed mode of behavior in the young child first learning to read. That is, attitudes related to interactional behavior between people are given greater emphasis than either attitudes which motivate individual behavior or describe what a

Table 10-3
**Frequency of Occurrence of the Attitudes Rated
for All Countries**

Attitude	Rank	Frequency
Caring, nurturing (b)[a]	1	428
Playing (B)	2	372
Presence of food or drink (A)[b]	3	318
Working (B)	4	303
Cleanliness, orderliness (C)[c]	5	169
Oldness, traditionalism (A)	6	166
Recognition of death or infirmity (A)	7	161
Imitation, role playing (B)	8	155
Physical aggression (B)	9	152
Education in schools (A)	10	134
Exploring, discovering (C)	11	130
Ambition, initiative (C)	12	108
Family togetherness (A)	13	102
Conforming, compromising (B)	14	90
Ignorance, incompetence (C)	15	88
Intelligence, alertness (C)	16	81
Religiousness (A)	17	78
Cruelty (B)	18	67
Physical strength (C)	19	64
Physical weakness (C)	20	64
Nationalism (A)	21	60
Dirtiness, disorderliness (C)	22	55
Competitiveness (B)	23	52
Selfishness, possessiveness (B)	24	50
Nonconforming, uncompromising (B)	25	47
Obedience in relation to authority (B)	26	46
Uncaring, neglecting (B)	27	41
Reference to economic transaction (A)	28	39
Recognition of cultural differences (A)	29	39
Cowardice (C)	30	38
Social regulation and structure (A)	31	36
Motor competency (C)	32	29
Lack of ambition, lassitude (C)	33	29
War, weaponry (A)	34	28
Disobedience in relation to authority (B)	35	28
Courage, bravery (C)	36	22
Independence (B)	37	21
Motor incompetency (C)	38	17
Peace (A)	39	7
Interactional passivity, no physical aggression (B)	40	5

[a] (B) Other-Directed Set. [b] (A) Cultural Set. [c] (C) Inner-Directed Set.

country is like. This statement is supported further by the data presented in Table 10-5, where in twelve of the thirteen countries, the greater percentage of attitudes presented are in the Other-Directed group. (These percentages represent the distribution of attitudes in 60 stories within a country according to the three groupings.) Only Israel has a slightly higher percentage of attitudes falling in the Cultural group column.

Returning to Table 10-3, one can observe the interval between attitude frequencies. A large interval exists between Working, ranked fourth, and Cleanliness and Orderliness, ranked fifth. The interval is 134, representing the difference between 303 and 169. Going down the table, attitudes appear at slightly varying intervals with the next largest interval occuring between Exploring and Discovering, ranked eleventh, and Ambition and Initiative, ranked twelfth. Examining these intervals provides an impression of which groups of attitudes are displayed frequently and which groups are not.

The last nine of the 40 attitudes in Table 10-3 show a frequency of below 30 out of a story sample of 780. These include Motor Competency (F=29), Lack of Ambition (F=29), War and Weaponry (F=28), Disobedience in Relation to Authority (F=28), Courage and Bravery (F=22), Independence (F=21), Motor Incompetency (F=17), Peace (F=7), and No Physical Aggression (F=5).

One wonders why these are given such little display. Recognizing these low frequencies and the frequency distribution of the other attitudes may call attention to what is being included and what is being left out. Hess and Torney (1967) stress that the school could make a more effective effort in developing attitudes and values about oneself, one's country, other nations, and how one should behave with others. Reading textbooks are one medium through which acculturation and socialization can take place in a school setting.

A note of caution should be made regarding the interpretation of these data. Since negative or positive valences were not placed on the presentation of the attitude in the stories as they were rated, it is not always possible to discuss the value good-bad, placed by the country on them. In other words, simply because an attitude is present in high frequency does not automatically suggest that it is always considered desirable. For example, the fact that the Presence of Food or Drink is in low frequency in the United States (F=15) might reflect that food is not an important issue because it is assumed to be in abundance.

Whereas in India, the high frequency of appearance of this attitude (F=35) is likely to reflect the recognized shortage of food in that country. Thus, in both countries, food may be highly valued though not equally stressed in stories written for beginning readers.

By using partitioned χ^2 (Castellan, 1965), it is possible to distinguish those countries which are significantly different from other countries in the frequency of occurrence of the attitudes rated. The attitudes which depicted the greatest difference between countries were Oldness, Playing, Working, Conforming, Presence of Food and Drink, Caring and Nurturing, and Cleanliness and Orderliness (see Table 10-4).

Oldness and Traditionalism intended to capture a story's orientation to the past, recognizing the influence of oldness or tradition on the present. It was relevant when an old person was present in the story and also relevant when customs or nonhuman items clearly referred to the past or oldness. The texts used in South Korea (F=42) and India (F=34) are very high in frequency of this attitude in the 60 stories; Turkey (F=3), Mexico (F=3), Russia (F=2), and the United States (F=1) are the lowest.

Playing refers to being actively engaged in recreation or sport, alone or with others. France includes Play most often (F=44), Israel mentions it least often (F=13). Nevertheless, both France (F=27) and Israel (F=24) include Working with approximately equal frequency.

Working was scored when animate characters were involved in roles for remuneration or when reference was made to an occupation. It was also considered present when remuneration was not involved but when the quality of "toiling" was, such as children doing chores or a father chopping wood for a campfire. Mexico (F=35), India (F=35), and South Korea (F=34) presented Working more often than the other countries, especially when compared to England (F=11) where the lowest frequency of this attitude appeared.

Conforming and Compromising was defined as adapting one's behavior to facilitate harmonious interaction in a way that was stronger than mere cooperation. A certain "giving in" was necessary. South Korea (F=22) and India (F=18) are high compared to the rest of the countries, with France (F=1) and the United States (F=0) having the lowest number of occurrences.

Caring and Nurturing referred to any character caring and helping another character. It was considered an action and distinguished from the affect of caring or love. This attitude is mentioned in over

Table 10-4

Comparison of Attitudes Among Countries Using Partitioned x^2

	Countries		
Attitude	High Frequency	Medium Frequency	Low Frequency
Oldness and Traditionalism	South Korea (42) India (34)	Japan (17) Israel (16) Italy (15)	West Germany (11) France (9) Norway (7) England (6) Turkey (3) Mexico (3) Russia (2) United States (1)
Play	France (44) South Korea (40) England (39) Mexico (36)	India (33) West Germany (32) Japan (29) Norway (28) United States (25)	Turkey (20) Russia (17) Italy (16) Israel (13)
Work	Mexico (35) India (35) South Korea (34)	France (27) Russia (25) Japan (25) Israel (24) Norway (22) United States (19)	Italy (17) Turkey (16) West Germany (13) England (11)
Conforming and Compromising	South Korea (22) India (18)	Norway (10) Italy (8)	Mexico (6) Russia (6) England (5) West Germany (5) Turkey (4) Japan (3) Israel (2) France (1) United States (0)
Caring and Nurturing	United States (45) India (44)	Mexico (37) South Korea (35) Turkey (33) England (32) Russia (31) Italy (31) Israel (30) Norway (30) Japan (30)	France (28) West Germany (22)

Table 10-4 (*continued*)

Attitude	High Frequency	Medium Frequency	Low Frequency
Presence of Food or Drink	India (35) France (29) Norway (29)	Turkey (28) Israel (27) England (26) West Germany (25) South Korea (25) Mexico (23)	Italy (21) Japan (19) Russia (16) United States (15)
Cleanliness and Orderliness	South Korea (49)		Turkey (16) West Germany (13) England (13) Japan (11) Mexico (10) France (9) India (9) Israel (9) Russia (9) Norway (8) Italy (7) United States (6)

two-thirds of the stories rated for both the United States (F=45) and India (F=44), as compared to approximately one-third of the stories from West Germany (F=22).

The Presence of Food or Drink, which refers to eating or any illustration or mention of food or drink for animals or humans, appears in over half of the stories from India (F=35) but in approximately one-quarter of the stories from Russia (F=16) and the United States (F=15).

South Korea (F=49) is outstandingly different from all other countries on the high frequency of the attitude of Cleanliness and Orderliness. This attitude refers to being free from dirt as well as clutter. Washing, sweeping, cleaning, straightening things out, setting objects in a sequence or in an orderly arrangement are all included. The remaining twelve countries are closely clustered together with frequencies approximating 25 percent or less of those rated in stories from South Korea.

Table 10-5 describes the percentage an attitude scale group occurred in the 60 stories for each of the thirteen countries. The

Cultural Posture group, which contains attitude scales that capture how people live in a particular country, shows the widest range of distribution, 30 percentage points. Israel, at the high end of the range (45 percent), differs significantly at the .01 level from Russia (21 percent), England (19 percent), and the United States (15 percent), at the lower end of the range.

Table 10-5

Percentage of Occurrence of Attitude Scale Groups for Each Country

Country	Cultural Posture Group	Other-Directed Posture Group	Inner-Directed Posture Group
England	19[a]	50	31[b]
France	31	55	14[a]
India	38	42[a]	20[a]
Israel	45[b]	40[a]	14[a]
Italy	29	46	25
Japan	29	49	22
Mexico	30	52	18[a]
Norway	28	47	25
Russia	21[a]	47	32
South Korea	36	46	18[a]
Turkey	33	45	22
United States	15[a]	56[b]	29
West Germany	29	44	26

[a]Denotes country where the attitude scale group is in significantly low frequency when compared to country marked[b] within a particular attitude scale group.
[b]Denotes country where the attitude scale group is in significantly higher frequency when compared to country marked[a] within a particular attitude scale group.

The narrowest distribution, 16 percentage points, is found in the Other-Directed Posture group, that is, attitude scales related to interactional behavior between people. The United States, at the higher end of the distribution (56 percent), differs significantly at the .01 level from India (42 percent), and Israel (40 percent) at the lower end of the range.

A spread of 18 percentage points is shown for the Inner-Directed Posture group, that is, attitude scales which contain attitudes that motivate or guide people's behavior. Stories from Russia (32 percent), and England (31 percent) are at the high end of the range and differ

Table 10-6

Frequency of Occurrence of Specific Attitudes—India and Israel

Cultural Posture	Other-Directed Posture	Inner-Directed Posture
Religiousness, devotion to God (H)	Role playing, learning, imitation (M)	Exploring, curiosity, discovering (L)
Recognition or portrayal of death or realistic danger, infirmity, illness, or injury (M)	Working, laboring, toiling (M)	Ambition, striving, aspiring, persistence, initiative (L)
Education in schools (M)	Uncaring, unhelping, neglecting, disregarding (L)	No ambition, lassitude, laziness (L)
Family togetherness (M)	Interactional physical aggression (L)	Motor incompetence, motor ineptness, clumsiness (L)
War, warfare, militarism, weaponry, (L)	Competitiveness, rivalry (L)	Cleanliness, orderliness, neatness (L)
Recognition of other countries' nationalities, ethnic groups, and cultures (L)	Selfishness, possessiveness, greediness, not sharing (L)	Dirtiness, disorderliness, untidiness, disorganization (L)
Peace, pacifism, armistice (L)	Nonconforming, uncompromising, unyielding, disagreeing, disputing (L)	Cowardice, lack of courage (L)
Social regulations and structure, social rules and laws (L)	Independence (L)	Courage, bravery, daring, boldness, fearlessness (L)
	Disobedience to authority (L)	Physical strength, powerfulness, brawniness (L)
	Cruelty, meanness, ruthlessness (L)	

111

Table 10-7

Frequency of Occurrence of Specific Attitudes—England, Russia, the United States

Cultural Posture	Other-Directed Posture	Inner-Directed Posture
Family togetherness (M)	Caring, helping, nurturing, protecting (H)	Exploring, curiosity, discovering (M)
Recognition or portrayal of death or realistic danger, infirmity, illness or injury (M)	Role playing, learning, imitation (M)	Cleanliness, orderliness, neatness (M)
Recognition of other countries' nationalities, ethnic groups and cultures (L)	Selfishness, possessiveness, greediness, not sharing (L)	Dirtiness, disorderliness, untidiness, disorganization (L)
War, warfare, militarism, weaponry (L)	Conforming, complying, compromising, conceding, acquiescing, consenting (L)	No ambition, lassitude, laziness (L)
Nationalism, patriotism (L)	Independence (L)	Cowardice, lack of courage (L)
Reference to economic transaction (L)	Obedience to authority (L)	Courage, bravery, daring, boldness, fearlessness (L)
Peace, pacifism, armistice (L)	Competitiveness, rivalry (L)	
	Interactional passtivity, no physical aggression (L)	
	Cruelty, meanness, ruthlessness (L)	

significantly [at the .01 level] from India (20 percent), South Korea (18 percent), Mexico (18 percent), France (14 percent), and Israel (14 percent) which fall at the low end of this range.

From Table 10-5, two subgroupings can be made, one of India and Israel, and the other of England, Russia, and the United States, in terms of their similarity to each other in their distribution over the three attitude scale groups. Using the distribution of specific attitudes from Table 10-4, similarities between India and Israel are illustrated in Table 10-6 and between England, Russia, and the United States in Table 10-7.

It should be noted that attitudes which are designated from Table 10-4 as being in high (H), medium (M), or low (L) frequency of occurrence in Tables 10-6 and 10-7, are based on the percentage range within each attitude scale group. Therefore, the designation high, medium, and low are only meaningful within each group and are not comparable between groups.

CONCLUSION

This study demonstrated that the content of first grade reading textbooks contain attitudes which can be reliably rated, given the reservation regarding the American-English cultural bias. Differences and similarities were found among these thirteen countries. Some descriptive highlights of the data have been presented. After more intensive analyses of the data, it should be possible to make further interpretations and inferences about differences and similarities among countries concerning national characteristics, moral systems, and child-rearing practices.

REFERENCES

Child, I. L., Porter, E. H., & Levine, E. M. "Children's textbooks and personality development: an exploration in the social psychology of education." *Psychological Monographs,* 1946, *60,* 1-54.

Castellan, N. J. "On the partitioning of contingency tables." *Psychological Bulletin,* 1965, *64,* 330-338.

Henry, J. "A cross national outline of education." *Current Anthropology,* 1960, *1,* 267-305.

Hess, R. D., & Torney, J. V. *The development of political attitudes in children*. Chicago: Aldine, 1967.

Holmes, M. B. "A cross cultural study of the relationship between values and modal conscience." In W. Muensterberger & S. Axelrad (eds.), *The psychoanalytic study of society*. Vol. 1. New York: International Universities Press, 1960.

McClelland, D. C. *The achieving society*. Princeton, N. J.: Van Nostrand, 1961.

CHAPTER 11

AGGRESSION AVOIDED — AGGRESSION NEEDED IN READING TEXTS

Sara Goodman Zimet

Since reading instruction is given top time priority each school day, the stories in reading textbooks provide teachers with a very valuable opportunity for dealing with the developmental interests and concerns of children and presenting to children a repertoire of models of socially adaptive behavior.

CONTENT OF READING TEXTBOOKS

That reading texts do contain behavior patterns and cultural expectations has been established by several investigators. Careful analyses of reading textbook content has revealed values related to economic development (de Charms & Moeller, 1962; McClelland,

This chapter first appeared, in its original version, as: Zimet, S. G. "A Rationale for the Inclusion of Aggression Themes in Elementary Reading Textbooks," *Psychology in the Schools*, 7: 232-37, 1970. Reprinted by permission.

1961), patterns of social behavior and social values (Anderson, 1956; Chilcott, 1961; Estensen, 1946; Mandel, 1964; Wargney, 1963), occupational and economic realities (Clyse, 1959; Stevens, 1941; Tennyson & Monnens, 1963-1964), cognitive and affective factors (Child, Potter, & Levine, 1946; Holmes, 1960), interest and motivational variables (see Chaps. 1 and 2), and sex role models (see Chap. 9). Common to most of these studies is the finding that in the texts most commonly used in the United States, the models presented are developmentally, culturally, and socially inappropriate. What is missing is "flesh-and-blood characters, faced with recognizable problems (who) win . . . the achievable goals or fail in an instructive way" (Jennings, 1965, p. 40).

We must utilize and capitalize on the school's role as a socializing agent and the reading textbook as a medium through which relevant material is transmitted. It may very well be that the degree of success which the reading text achieves as a socializing agent is directly related to its success as an instrument of instruction. As Asheim (1956) has said, so long as action seems more desirable in our society than thought, and rewards from any time-consuming activity must be tangible and immediate, and reading is so difficult to learn, it is going to be extremely difficult to convince more than a few in our society that reading has a justifiable claim on their time.

EFFECT OF READING

The socializing effect of reading may be explained in terms of the processes of identification and ego development. Identification is the process that leads the individual to mold his own behavior after one whom he has taken as a model. The individual endeavors to think, feel, or behave as though the characteristics of another person or group of people belong to him. In this sense, stories project characters and events upon the reader who in turn projects himself onto the characters and events in the stories.

It has been said that reading "is the art of transmitting the ideas, facts, and feelings from the mind and soul of an author to the mind and soul of a reader" (Jennings, 1965, p. 11). Reading also offers the individual the opportunity to widen the boundaries of his ego and to strive towards a better integration of his life experiences (Pickard, 1959). In other words, as the child reads, he matches his view of the world about him with the one presented in the story. The degree of congruence the story has with his perceptions of reality will facilitate this integration and determine the extent to which his ego boundaries are expanded. Thus, for the child, reading should quickly become a major instrument for the management of his universe. Things happen to him because he reads, and he reads further because of what happens.

Friedlander (1942) and Peller (1959) explain from a psychoanalytic viewpoint that books exercise their power of attraction on latency age children through their emotional content. Favorite stories contain some universal fantasies and defense mechanisms which are characteristic of the child's development at the beginning of the latency period. They go on to state that when a story is appropriate to the particular stage of development of the child, it can definitely help the child to overcome his conflicts.

The hypothesis that books help children face and solve problems arising from everyday life has been tested and supported by several investigators (Bender & Lourie, 1941; Cianciolo, 1965; Martin, 1955; Mattera, 1961; Witty, 1964). There appears to be unanimous agreement among them, however, that those stories which do effect attitudes and behavior vary enormously from individual to individual. Children's choices of books and responses to these books are dependent upon idiosyncratic personality characteristics and needs. Thus, reading for children as well as for adults is a private, unique experience. The reading fare, therefore, in order to be truly syntonic with life, must be varied enough to provide opportunities to focus on meaningful issues and solutions to problems as well as to offer necessary comic relief when confrontations become too intense and threatening. Both the universals of childhood, of which Friedlander and Peller speak, and the idiosyncratic ones that distinguish one individual from another, need to find their way into the themes of elementary reading textbooks.

AGGRESSION IN CHILDREN

Bender (1953) arrived at a developmental picture of aggressive behavior starting with the infant's experimentation and exploration of objects in the external world, both animate and inanimate, to gain a sense of power and mastery of his world. "Considerable aggressiveness is essential in the psychology of the child or else it would be impossible for it to break the ties of dependency, strike out on its own, and achieve personal autonomy and the foundation of a new family" (Storr, 1968, p. 50).

It has also been noted, through controlled observations of their play and interpersonal relationships (Ames, 1966; Bender, 1953; Korner, 1949; Sears, Rau, & Alpert, 1965), and through analysis of their own stories (Pitcher & Prelinger, 1963), that preschool children manifest aggressive and even violent behavior. "Aggression . . . springs from an innate tendency to grow and master life which seems to be characteristic of all living matter. Only when this life force is obstructed in its development do ingredients of anger, rage, or hate become connected with it" (Thompson, 1964, p. 179).

In *Children Tell Stories*, Pitcher and Prelinger (1963) attribute the frequent recurrence of themes of aggression, hurt, misfortune, and death in stories told by nursery school children to the existence of aggressive impulses, a concern with suffering physical harm, as well as to the loss of a secure sense of self.

Aggression, next to dependency, is judged to be the most indulged behavior in a middle-class society (Whiting & Child, 1964). Parents allow somewhat more aggression from their sons than from their daughters. However, working-class parents are less permissive about aggression within the family structure than middle-class parents (Sears, Maccoby, & Levin, 1957), but more permissive in accepting aggressive behavior as a way to solve problems with those outside the family unit. As a matter of fact, aggressive behavior is one facet of the socialization process which is an object of concern to both parents and to professionals who work with children. It is one of the most frequent behavior problems for which children are referred to outpatient clinics (Patterson, Littman & Bricker, 1967). In addition, several researchers have found that children who have unusual difficulty in learning to read are often children who have great difficulty handling the aggression that is a normal part of growing up (Rubenstein, Falick, & Ekstein, 1959; Walsh, 1956).

Whether aggression is determined by social or biological characteristics (Berkowitz, 1962; Storr, 1968), it is generally agreed that learning can affect an individual's reaction to aggression-arousing situations and learning can govern the exact form of the aggressive reaction. "When angered, a seventeenth century nobleman might automatically reach for his sword, a nineteenth century cowboy for his gun, and a twentieth century Englishman for his pen so he could write to the London *Times*" (Berkowitz, 1962, pp. 34-35).

AGGRESSION IN AMERICA

The legend of American aggressiveness finds substantiation in history starting with the hardships faced by the colonists in settling a new land, fighting many wars, and pushing frontiers westward. The establishment of the United States as a major economic and political force in the world in a relatively short period of time could not have been accomplished without a high degree of aggressiveness.

Today the United States has the "dubious distinction of being the most lawless of the world's nations" (Dickinson, 1969, p. 49). Race riots, student riots, the Vietnam war, crime on the streets, death on the highways, the assassination of three major national leaders, and the threat of atomic annihilation are flashed and screamed across the mass media within view and earshot of the very youngest as well as the very oldest.

A look at the entertainment media for young people tells us even more about the emphasis on violence in American life. "T.V. for children is a mass of indiscriminate entertainment dominated by some forty animated program series distinguished for ugliness, noise, and violence" (Dickinson, 1969, p. 50). On the movie screens and in the comic books, scenes of fighting, slugging, beating, torturing, clubbing, and shooting abound (Menninger, 1968; Wertham, 1953). Wertham characterizes our present era as having the greatest potential for violence—technologically, socially, psychologically, and politically. He concludes that we are in the "age of violence" (p. 13). Storr (1968) agrees. "We are threatened," he says, "as a species by our own destructiveness, and we shall never learn to control this unless we understand ourselves better" (p. 122).

AGGRESSION IN READING TEXTS

The existence of man's aggressiveness has been fully recognized and documented by history, the mass media, and the behavioral sciences, but stories in first and third grade reading textbooks infrequently present aggression themes (Child et al., 1946; Zimet, 1968). When they do, they give the impression that aggression is merely a deplorable impulse experienced only by animals, supernatural creatures, and villainous children or adults, rather than an integral part of man's life which is capable of serving him in constructive as well as destructive ways.

There was a general absence of either training or cathartic value in the presentation of aggressive behavior in the third grade reading textbooks coded by Child et al. (1946). The authors noted that child aggression ranked sixteenth out of the twenty-three categories listed, with adult fairy characters as most aggressive and animal characters following in second place. Despite its low frequency of appearance in the stories, aggression was the most often punished of all forms of behavior found in the readers. Thus, to the child reading these stories, the behavior was detached enough so that he would not copy it and yet plausible enough for him to accept the moral that aggressive behavior leads to punishment. In this way, two purposes were served: (1) to avoid the necessity of showing child characters as exhibiting undesirable behavior, and (2) to present an object lesson demonstrating the results of such behavior when manifested (Zimet, 1968). In other words, children are not known as having aggressive feelings which often get them into conflicts with parents, siblings, friends, neighbors, teachers, etc., and obviously neither are they shown ways of resolving these conflicts constructively.

The neglect given to positive aggressive drives in both first and third grade readers has also been described by these same investigators. Child et al. (1946) found that independent action initiated by child characters and indeed by anyone, was more likely to be punished than similar behavior performed under the direction of a superior. For example, self-initiated pursuit of knowledge through the child's own explorations was frequently punished, whereas knowledge gained through dependence upon authority was almost always rewarded.

A parallel situation was described by Zimet (1968) who noted that there was a significantly high incidence of dependence in the first grade texts coded and that this behavior was rewarded overwhelmingly for both sexes and all age levels. Interestingly enough, the dependency model for the male was even more striking in frequency than for the female. Not only are these characterizations of dependency behavior not congruent with the behavior expectations of society at large, but they are also developmentally inappropriate.

CONCLUSION

There is a vital role that elementary reading textbooks can perform in overcoming the discontinuities between childhood and adulthood, life in school and in the world outside school. By dealing with aggressive drives directly, the child can better understand both the direction these drives can take him and the direction he can take them. By combining the talents of the artist-writer and the understanding of the behavioral scientist, it may be possible to write textbooks that are equally effective as instruments of acculturation and of teaching the reading skill. As Pickard (1959) has stated, nothing is too bad for children to hear since terrible basic plots are already within and without him. What matters is how they hear about these things.

REFERENCES

Ames, L. B. "Children's stories." *Genetic Psychology Monographs*, 1966, *73*, 337-396.

Anderson, P. S. "McGuffey vs. modern in character training." *Phi Delta Kappa*, 1956, *38*, 136-142.

Asheim, L. "What do adults read?" In N. B. Henry (ed.), *Adult reading*. 55th Yearbook of the National Society for the Study of Education, Part II. Chicago: University of Chicago Press, 1956, pp. 5-28.

Bender, L. *Aggression, hostility, and anxiety in children*. Springfield, Ill.: Charles C. Thomas, 1953.

Bender, L., & Lourie, R. "The effect of comic books on the ideology of children." *American Journal of Orthopsychiatry*, 1941, *11*, 540-550.

Berkowitz, L. *Aggression: a social psychological analysis.* New York: McGraw-Hill, 1962.

Chilcott, J. H. "An analysis of the enculturation of values as illustrated in primary readers of 1879-1960." Paper read at the California Educational Research Association Meeting, Palo Alto, Cal., March 4, 1961.

Child, I. L., Potter, E. H., & Levine, E. M. "Children's textbooks and personality development: an exploration in the social psychology of education." *Psychological Monographs*, 1946, *60*, 1-54.

Cianciolo, P. J. "Children's literature can affect coping behavior." *Personnel and Guidance Journal*, 1965, *43*, 897-903.

Clyse, J. "What do basic readers teach about jobs?" *Elementary School Journal*, 1959, *59*, 456-460.

de Charms, R., & Moeller, G. H. "Values expressed in American children's readers." *Journal of Abnormal and Social Psychology*, 1962, *64*, 136-142.

Dickinson, W. B., Jr. (ed.), *Editorial research reports on urban environment.* Washington: Congressional Quarterly, 1969.

Estensen, E. V. "McGuffey—a statistical analysis." *Journal of Educational Research*, 1946, *34*, 445-456.

Friedlander, K. "Children's books and their function in latency and prepuberty." *American Imago*, 1942, *3*, 129-150.

Holmes, M. B. "A cross-cultural study of the relationship between values and modal conscience." In W. Muensterberger & S. Axelrad (eds.), *The psychoanalytic study of society*. Vol. 1. New York: International Universities Press, 1960, pp. 98-181.

Jennings, F. G. *This is reading.* New York: Teachers College, Columbia University, 1965.

Korner, A. F. *Some aspects of hostility in young children.* New York: Grune & Stratton, 1949.

Mandel, R. L. "Children's books: mirrors of social development." *Elementary School Journal*, 1964, *64*, 190-199.

Martin, C. "But how do books help children?" *Junior Libraries*, 1955, *1*, 83-87.

Mattera, G. "Bibliotherapy in a sixth grade." Unpublished doctoral dissertation, Pennsylvania State University, 1961.

McClelland, D. D. *The achieving society.* Princeton, N. J.: Van Nostrand, 1961.

Menninger, K. "The crime of punishment." *Saturday Review*, September 7, 1968, pp. 21-25, 55.

Patterson, G. R., Littman, R. A., & Bricker, W. "Assertive behavior in children: a step toward a theory of aggression." *Monograph of the Society for Research in Child Development*, 1967, *32*, 1-43.

Peller, L. E. "Daydreams and children's favorite books." In R. S. Eissler, A. Freud, H. Hartmann, & M. Kris (eds.), *The psychoanalytic study of the child*. New York: International Universities Press, 1959, pp. 414-433.

Pickard, P. M. *I could a tale unfold.* London: Tavistock Publications, 1959.

Pitcher, E. G., & Prelinger, E. *Children tell stories: an analysis of fantasy.* New York: International Universities Press, Inc., 1963.

Rubenstein, B. O., Falick, M. L., & Ekstein, R. "Learning impotence: a suggested diagnostic category." *American Journal of Orthopsychiatry*, 1959, *29*, 315-323.

Sears, R. R., Maccoby, E. E., & Levin, H. *Patterns of child rearing*. Evanston, Ill.: Row, Peterson, 1957.

Sears, R. R., Rau, L., & Alpert, R. *Identification and child rearing*. Stanford, Cal.: Stanford University Press, 1965.

Stevens, L. "Format and content of readers." *Elementary School Journal*, 1941, *42*, 120-129.

Storr, A. *Human aggression*. New York: Atheneum, 1968.

Tennyson, W. W., & Monnens, L. P. "The world of work through elementary readers." *Vocational Guidance Quarterly*, Winter 1963-1964, 85-88.

Thompson, C. M. *Interpersonal psychoanalysis*. New York: Basic Books, 1964.

Walsh, A. M. *Self-concepts of bright boys with learning difficulties*. New York: Teachers College, Columbia University, 1956.

Wargney, F. O. "The good life in modern readers." *The Reading Teacher*, 1963, *17*, 88-93.

Wertham, F. *Seduction of the innocent*. New York: Rinehart, 1953.

Wertham, F. *A sign for Cain*. New York: Macmillan, 1966.

Whiting, J. W. M., & Child, I. L. *Child training and personality: a cross-cultural study*. New Haven, Conn.: Yale University Press, 1964.

Witty, P. A. "Meeting developmental needs through reading." *Education*, 1964, *84*, 451-458.

Zimet, S. G. "Sex role models in primary reading texts of the United States: 1600-1966." Unpublished doctoral dissertation, University of Denver, 1968.

CHAPTER 12

THE CHILD WONDERS:
READING FOR WHAT?

Sara Goodman Zimet

Next to one's family and peers, the school is capable of exercising significant influence over the lives of children.

Beginning with Kindergarten or first grade, the center of the child's extra-familial life, occupying almost half of his waking hours, is the school. The kind of teachers he has, the teaching methods he encounters, and the types of textbooks he is exposed to will have important effects not only on his progress but upon his capacity to meet and master new problems and challenges and, consequently, his self-confidence and self-esteem (Mussen, Conger, & Kagan, 1969, pp. 587-588).

And yet, the meaninglessness of school experience to the student throughout the country has been documented time and time again. It has been established that, increasingly, from the elementary grades upwards through college, schooling has little pertinence to what is of real concern and interest to students and that there is little connection between what they need and what they get (Jersild, Lazar, & Brodkin, 1962). Today this lack of relevance of many of our educational experiences is being actively challenged by college and high school youth across our nation through petitions, parades, sit-ins, talk-outs, as well as through other less acceptable confrontations with school administrations. The activism of today's challengers is in sharp contrast to the passivity displayed by past generations. Traditionally, if one found a lack of pertinence in his educational experience, he would do one of two things, accept his plight and conform to expectations or drop out. For the high school student, dropping out completely only became possible at the age of sixteen. But an examination of students' records usually shows that they dropped out psychologically by the end of the second grade at the latest and have been attending school under protest ever since. Junior high and elementary school students, therefore, share the feelings of their older counterparts without necessarily sharing the same form of protest.

Although the first grade student does not express disappointment with his educational experience in antiestablishment terms, the disappointment is still there and is frequently manifested in failure, a mode well within the bounds of society's expectations judging by the practice of retention and the development of elementary school remediation specialists and centers within the schools. Each year from 2 to 10 percent of children become nonpromotion statistics (*Reading disorders*, 1969). When the child is retained in the first grade, he suffers a public defeat and humiliation in his own eyes and in those of his family and his peers. Usually he will experience the misery of such a failure once or twice again by the seventh grade (Stickney, 1969). But rather than getting used to the continuous consequences of failing, such a child develops apathy and a feeling of worthlessness. Such feelings become an integral part of his personality makeup (Spache, 1957; Walsh, 1956). When children who are failing continue to be promoted with their classmates despite their inability to keep up with the work, they often drop out of school eventually and later fail in society (*Reading disorders*, 1969).

And what has all this to do with reading? The vast majority of school failures began with reading difficulties and the most frequent cause of retention is reading failure (*Reading disorders*, 1969). Since one must read in order to master other subjects, the troubles multiply and the failures increase. A closer look at recent figures describing the extent and magnitude of the problem may help to put the issue into its proper perspective.

Reading disorders affect about 15 percent of the children in schools today (Peltola, 1963). But more specifically, 91 out of 100 children in the sixth grade in Newark, N. J., schools cannot read adequately. Language disorders affect at least 10 percent of school children, 50 percent of school dropouts and 90 percent of juvenile delinquents (*Reading disorders*, 1969). A study of ninth grade students in the New York City schools in 1965 indicated that 50.1 percent were shown by tests to be below grade level in reading, and 35 percent two or more grade levels below (*Reading disorders*, 1969). In view of these figures, it is certainly worth repeating a comment made by a principal of a Harlem elementary school, that a child's not reading is his first step toward alienation from the society in which he lives (Stickney, 1969).

Familiarity with adult reading behavior also throws light on the issue. In spite of our relatively high level of education, we Americans by and large are not serious readers. The typical American does not read much beyond billboards, daily tabloid newspapers, instructions on how-to-do-it packets and other similar material (Grambs, 1959). Somewhat less than half our adult population reads below the ninth grade level: one-third of these are functional illiterates, or those known as nonreaders (Stickney, 1969). Functional literates, those persons completing fewer than five years of schooling, make up 11 percent of our population (Gray, 1956).

There are even those students who play the learning game to the point of acquiring the basic reading skills without acquiring the desire to read. These students pass reading achievement tests successfully but never read beyond what is required by the teacher when they are in school and not at all in their adult years. Here we have achievement-test literacy, where reading has only served to get students through but has never served any other useful purpose in their lives. This is aptly demonstrated by the fact that reading, book buying, and book borrowing from libraries show a significant drop at the school leaving point. Those who leave school after completing high school virtually stop all reading except newspapers and magazines. This is also true for those who go on and graduate from college. Those adults who remain in academia continue to read for specific and tangible ends and not for its own sake. Reading is undertaken when some immediate reward can be forseen (Asheim, 1960).

Initial experiences in the elementary school must certainly play a large role in people's attitudes toward reading and books. Children who learn to read with ease and satisfaction in their first year of schooling probably develop into lifetime readers. But students who find reading a punishing and threatening experience can hardly be expected to read with great interest and enthusiasm.

How then can a first grade reading instruction program create the desire to read? One extremely important but frequently neglected solution brings us back to the issue of "meaningfulness" discussed at the beginning of this chapter. Schools should help students to master intellectual skills and to pass tests of academic achievement. But, in addition, schools must help the student to incorporate what he learns into a realistic view of himself, helping him to effectively meet the internal and external demands which arise in the process of growing up. These objectives emphasize personal meaning. Unfortunately curriculum materials that might be rich in personal implications frequently avoid them and the subjects are taught and learned in a mechanical way. The same is true of primary reading textbooks. Reading texts emphasize skill, and reading is taught for the sake of the skill itself. We need to shift our emphasis from "reading to learn to read" to "reading about something meaningful while learning to read." By emphasizing process to the exclusion of meaningful ideas, we sacrifice the raison d'etre for learning to read. It has already been ascertained that young beginning readers have serious difficulty in understanding the purpose of written language (Downing, 1969; Reid, 1966).

When children are taught verbal rules about reading they learn that reading is a kind of ritual which they have to perform to please adults. They also learn that reading and writing are dull and boring tasks which have little or nothing to do with the interesting things in their lives outside school. Thus many children take a very long time to learn the essential truth about reading which is that it is to convey interesting information from the author to the reader (Downing, 1969, p. 227).

The trouble lies in the fact that the sounds of words as well as the spoken words themselves are meaningless sounds for so many beginning readers. In order for reading to be the translation from written symbols to that form of language to which the child already attaches meaning, there must be simultaneous use of language on three levels: phonemic, syntactic, and semantic (Niensted, 1969). Acceptance of written words as representations of reality will depend on how closely they resemble the lifespace of the six-year-old since meaning rests in experience. Both the fantasy and reality of children's lives are full and rich compared to the pallid scenes and words found in the beginning reading texts. The need to include the physical, emotional, cognitive, and aesthetic here-and-now of their world will help bridge the gap between process and purpose in reading instruction.

In an informal survey of college textbooks on reading instruction used by prospective elementary school teachers, none were found that described the content of ideas of reading texts or discussed the possible influence of this content on learning to read. Most of them recognized that "interest is the touchstone of reading achievement" but the development of an interest in reading was viewed as dependent upon an environment external to the textbooks themselves. This finding stimulated a curiosity as to the extent that publishers of beginning reading series were interested in the story content. In an effort to discover the answer to this, the author wrote to the publishers of the eleven most widely used reading textbooks asking them if they set up specific criteria for use by the authors writing the stories for inclusion in these texts.

Answers were received from eight of the eleven publishers and none claimed to have any preestablished criterion. Seven of the eight respondents did state, however, that they depended very much on the expertise of their authors and advisers who were experienced teachers and reading specialists. The assumption that experienced teachers and reading specialists are best suited to writing interesting stories for inclusion in texts for beginning readers has little support in the literature. As a matter of fact, it has been established that authoritative adult sources are frequently in error with regard to what children really select and enjoy in literary material (Kolson, Robinson, & Zimmerman, 1962; Norvell, 1958; Peltola, 1963). And yet several of the respondents went so far as to state that it would be presumptuous of them to interfere with the authors' selections and that authors should be free to perform more creative and original work without the imposition of specific criteria imposed upon them by the publishers.

Perhaps it is safe to assume that external standards and strict guidelines could hamper the writers' ability to write stories for reading textbooks. But if we accept at face value what has been stated above, and examine the degree that the authors of these texts have achieved "creative and original work," what we discover is that there is an amazing and consistent similarity found in all of the major series published.

It is worth noting that a publisher's investment might well be over a million dollars and approximately six years of continuous effort before a reading textbook series is ready for marketing (Jennings, 1965). In order to protect this enormous investment of time and money, publishers need and want system-wide if not state-wide adoptions. Anything which might threaten the acceptability of the series is omitted. This may well account for the dependence upon a content formula which has proven acceptable in the past.

Thus, we should hardly be surprised to observe that what seems to be playing an important and obviously stifling role in deciding the content of the primers is "tradition." Since around 1930, a pattern of textbook content and format has been established and maintained. Exceptions have been minor. In stating that the criteria used in the past would scarcely be suitable for today's materials, one of the publishers obviously could not have been referring to the substantive and motivational content of the stories. In all likelihood he was referring to such factors as vocabulary control and gradation, and the structure of words and sentences.

The persistence with which these textbook stories are placed in a rural-suburban setting also may be attributable to "tradition." Information from the first census which was taken in 1790, placed only 5 percent of the nation's inhabitants in the city. From 1810 on, the rural population decreased until the balance was tipped by 1920. As a matter of fact, ever since metropolitan areas were first reported in the 1910 census their rate of population growth has far exceeded that for the country as a whole (Dickinson, 1969). Thus, in reviewing the environmental settings of stories in reading texts in wide use during the period from 1835 to 1966 (see Table 12-1), one finds that what may have been the "here-and-now" for the school child of 1835 became the "no-man's-land" for many children by 1966.

A similar situation exists in the presentation of the primary story characters as being white Anglo-Saxon middle-class types. Over 32 million people immigrated to the United States between 1840 and 1911

Table 12-1

Environmental Place Settings in Primary Reading Textbooks
Used in the United States from 1835-1966 (Percentages)

	Rural	*Suburban*	*Urban*	*Other/Not Clear*
1835-1898	40	0	8	52
1898-1921	40	0	1	59
1921-1940	18	40	11	31
1940-1966	10	67	9	14

Source: Zimet, S. G., "Sex role models in primary reading texts of the United States: 1600-1966." Unpublished doctoral dissertation, University of Denver, 1968.

(Dickinson, 1969), and today, across the country, 6,340,000 nonwhite children are learning to read and understand the American way of life in books which either omit them entirely or scarcely mention them (Larrick, 1965).

A statement found in teacher's guides accompanying primer series was also repeated by one of the respondents when he said that stories of high literary quality are included in the texts. None of the textbook authors have established themselves as writers of fiction or nonfiction. No Caldecott or Newberry* awards have been earned by these texts. As a matter of fact, none of the stories have ever been scrutinized and judged by any literary critics.

In spite of the fact that over 40 percent of the content of primary reading texts are illustrations, none of the publishers made any reference to the selection of illustrative material. Color illustrations predominate in the texts examined. This is consistent with the preferences of young readers (Amsden, 1960). From a study of children's preferences of illustrative style and picture theme (Bloomer, 1960), the author recommended that when pictures are to stimulate interest and produce realistic thought about a subject, they should be line drawings with incomplete action themes related to the subject. But when pictures are to stimulate fantasy, they should be presented in color. Considering the discrepancy between the reality of children's

*The Caldecott award is given once a year to an American author for the most distinguished contribution to American literature for children. The Newberry is awarded annually to an illustrator for the most attractive illustrations in an American children's book.

lives and the themes presented in their reading textbooks, one might very well conclude that the color illustrations found in such profusion in the texts are well suited to do their job!

What appears to be needed is a break with traditional patterns of textbook writing and publishing. If it is true that textbook writers will write the books that publishers will accept and that publishers will accept the books that school boards will adopt and that school boards will adopt the books that organized public opinion will demand, then public opinion needs to be aroused to the desperate need for books that display and celebrate our national diversity, our pluralism, and, in fact, that life is not always a sun-drenched Sunday afternoon (Jennings, 1965).

The content of stories has importance regardless of the method of instruction. It would seem advisable that in preparing stories for primary reading texts, talented storytellers, artists, and specialists in child development join together in an effort with experienced teachers and reading specialists. This approach would take us a long way toward providing first graders with instructional materials that have a difficulty range and an interest appeal commensurate with children's cognitive and affective developmental levels.

REFERENCES

Amsden, R. H., "Children's preferences in picture story book variables." *Journal of Educational Research*, 1960, *53*, 309-312.

Asheim, L., "What do adults read?" In N. B. Henry (ed.), *Adult reading*, 55th Yearbook of the National Society for the Study of Education, Part II. Chicago: University of Chicago Press, 1956, pp. 5-28.

Bloomer, R. H., "Children's preference and responses as related to styles and themes of illustrations." *Elementary School Journal*, 1960, *60*, 334-340.

Dickinson, W. B., Jr. (ed.), *Editorial research reports on urban environment*. Washington: Congressional Quarterly, 1969.

Downing, J., "How children think about reading." *Reading Teacher*, 1969, *23*, 217-230.

Grambs, J. D., "The conference on lifetime reading habits," *Reading Teacher*, 1959, *12*, 218-221.

Gray, W. S., "How well do adults read?" In N. B. Henry (ed.), *Adult reading*, 55th Yearbook of the National Society for the Study of Education, Part II. Chicago: University of Chicago Press, 1956, pp. 29-56.

Jennings, F. G., *This is reading*. New York: Teachers College, Columbia University, 1965.

Jersild, A. T., Lazar, E. A., & Brodkin, A. M., *The meaning of psychotherapy in the teacher's life and work.* New York: Teachers College, Columbia University, 1962.

Kolson, C. J., Robinson, R. E., & Zimmerman, W. G., "Children's preferences in publishers." *Education*, 1962, *88*, 155-157.

Larrick, N., "The all-white world of children's books." *Saturday Review*, September 11, 1965, pp. 63-64, 84-85.

Mussen, P., Conger, J., & Kagan, J., *Child development and personality.* New York: Harper & Row, 1969.

Niensted, S., "Meaninglessness for beginning readers." *Reading Teacher,* 1969, *23*, 112-115.

Norvell, G. W., *What boys and girls like to read.* Morristown, N. J.: Silver Burdett, 1958.

Peltola, B. J., "A study of children's book choices," *Elementary English*, 1963, *40*, 690-696, 702.

Reading disorders in the United States. Report of the Secretary's (HEW) National Advisory Committee on Dyslexia and Related Reading Disorders. Washington: U. S. Dept. of Health, Education & Welfare, August, 1969.

Reid, F., "Learning to think about reading." *Educational Research*, 1966, *9*, 56-62.

Spache, G., "Personality patterns of retarded readers." *Journal of Educational Research*, 1957, *50*, 461-469.

Stickney, S. B., "Reading and childhood ecology." In *Conference on reading*, University of Pittsburgh Report No. 24. Pittsburgh: University of Pittsburgh Press, 1969, pp. 109-118.

Walsh, A. M., *Self-concepts of bright boys with learning difficulties.* New York: Teachers College, Columbia University, 1956.

Zimet, S. G., "Sex role models in primary reading texts of the United States: 1600-1966." Unpublished doctoral dissertation, University of Denver, 1968.

CHAPTER 13

RECOMMENDATIONS:
TO WHOM IT MAY CONCERN

Sara G. Zimet and Gaston E. Blom

The conclusion reached by the various research studies reported in this book is that reading should serve recognizable functions for first grade children. For this to be accomplished, the content of stories needs to be varied enough to appeal to the many reasons for reading: reading to learn about oneself and others, reading for information, reading for fun, and reading for escape. The following paragraphs discuss each of these reasons in the context of what kind of content should be included in first grade reading textbooks. Basic to the discussion is the conviction that textbook story writers need not be limited by outdated readability formulas or stilted syntax. The real life-space of first graders can be infused into the illustrations, vocabulary, and style of these beginning reading materials without sacrificing sound instructional methods and learning principles. Furthermore, the dichotomy between the *why* and the *how* of reading needs to be minimized, for regardless of reading method (the *how*), content (the *why*) counts.

Reading to Learn About Oneself and Others

Themes dealing with realistic issues of concern to first graders belong in reading textbooks. For some six-year-olds, entering the new world of the school is leaving the protective influence of the home and the neighborhood. For others, it involves expectancies that are far different than what they have been used to. In the school setting, the six-year-old is part of a large group of many unfamiliar faces and new authority figures who behave differently from any he has known before. The uniqueness of this situation frequently causes anxiety and confusion.

Specific measures which are aimed at bridging the discontinuities between home and school are important facilitators of school adjustment and learning. Textbook story content which presents a variety of anxiety-laden and unique experiences similar to what the first grader is experiencing is one such specific measure that can be psychologically helpful as well as instructional. For example, by presenting age-appropriate characters who are resourceful and clever and whose actions result in success, first graders might feel that they have control over circumstances which create anxiety and confusion and that they are able to successfully adapt to them.

Families are not always intact, nor is family life exclusively child-centered. Parents punish and children display a range of affects. Sibling rivalry, parent-child conflicts, birth and death, fears, accomplishments, failures—all are a part of the life-space of the first grade child. These issues are vital story material that can provide a repertoire of possible outcomes where they are successfully resolved sometimes, unsuccessfully resolved at other times, and even left unresolved occasionally. Such stories also provide reassurance that others are like oneself or experience what one has experienced. Or they may foster understanding that circumstances are different for other children. In either case, in story form, emotional distance is possible (i.e., this is not me; it is like me), and thereby lends a perspective to problems and situations that directly concern the reader.

Despite the cry for textbooks about real people from various ethnic, religious, and social class groups in a variety of environmental settings which are representative of America's diversity, there still appears to be a reluctance, with rare exception, to drop the traditional characterizations of unreal, middle-class, affluent, well-dressed, suburban, stereotyped-named, white, Protestant, affectless, middle-Americans. In effect, this represents a form of naive censorship, of keeping from children what they actually know exists—a kind of "let's not talk about or read about it and it will all go away" attitude. Yet, in reality, here is an excellent opportunity to present stories which acknowledge and depict people who are both alike and different from the reader—alike in feeling anxiety and joy, though different in cultural identity. People, both adults and children—whatever their ethnic, national, religious or social class identity may be—need to be humanized and identifiable, need to display a familiar range of emotions, both negative and positive, and need to behave in recognizable ways.

Animals should not be the only ones that carry the burden of displaying negative affects. They need to be characterized as animals—not primarily as anthropomorphized humans. Furthermore, pets need to assume the stature they deserve by presenting them in other than primarily nuisance and disruptive roles. They are attached to people and people to them. All animals have a life-style of their own. They give birth; they die; they are, at times, dependent, at other times, independent; they have likes and dislikes—all within the context of being animal. For example, dogs are companions, watchdogs, herders, and objects of love and fear. These characterizations are as interesting and appealing to first graders as are those depicted by the *Cat in the Hat* and *Yertle the Turtle*. There is a place for a variety of animal species and characterizations in primary textbook stories.

In accomplishing the developmental task of establishing a sexual identity, the growing child makes extensive use of identification with adults and older children. Thus, a more balanced distribution of characters of different ages and of both sexes, involved in a greater variety of age-appropriate activities is strongly recommended. For example, stories concerning the functions of adults (other than being parents) need to be present in far greater numbers than currently exist. Occupational, recreational and social adult models outside the family setting have been virtually absent from these texts.

The importance of presenting clearly definable masculine and feminine roles has been emphasized in several chapters throughout this book. Herein lies a danger—that of replacing the diffuse sex role model with a stereotyped, conventional male and female model and thereby perpetuating the culturally conditioned separateness that leads both boys and girls to devalue that which is feminine and to strive for that which is masculine. Stereotypes, whether they be national, ethnic, religious, social class, or gender, are inadequate to capture the fullness and richness that is or can be. Thus, the recommendation here is that the emphasis be placed "on being human"—on replacing old cliches associated with maleness and femaleness which help foster the inequities between the sexes in our society. One way to accomplish this is to present sex-disassociated career possibilities and role functions to children as young as first graders long before they begin to accept the stereotyped sex-role work and home models as unchangeable facts of life.

Interpersonal and work roles for both sexes should reflect *what is* as well as *what should be*. For example, women characters would be engineers, doctors, reporters, scientists, taxi drivers, letter carriers, secretaries, teachers, nurses and store clerks, *as well as* mothers, maiden aunts, sisters and daughters. On the other hand, men would be nurses, teachers, secretaries, cooks, waiters, store clerks, lawyers, mechanics, and carpenters, *as well as* fathers, bachelor uncles, brothers, and sons. Inside the home, married and/or unmarried women and men would both carry out the household and/or nurturant roles in a way that would not detract from a man's competence or emphasize a woman's incompetence.

Reading for Information

As was discovered in many story preference studies, informational content is sought by first graders. Children want to know the what, where, how and why of their world. This knowledge helps to order and make manageable much that is confusing and mysterious and to satisfy curiosities as well. Where things come from and go to—from food products to waste products—can be explored, e.g., milk, water, babies, wool, tin cans, paper, paint, etc. Also included in this category are descriptions of how things work—things such as toilets, motors, light switches, and thermometers.

Another source of informational content relates to the child's need to acquire and master new skills. How-to-do-it, be it cooking pudding, baking cookies, constructing simple scientific instruments, jumping rope, planting a small garden, or caring for a new pet, provide appropriate fare for the first grader.

Reading for Fun

Coincidentally, "fun" makes up the first three letters of the word "functional," and provides another avenue through which reading can serve the first grader. Thus, pranks, riddles, jokes, jingles, nonsense rhymes, cartoons, and comics all belong in the repertoire of primary reading textbooks. They are pleasurable in themselves, but the pleasure evoked from reading this material may also help to create positive and joyful associations with the learning-to-read process.

Reading for Escape

"Fantasy-promoting" and "adventuresome" were the words used to describe some of the most preferred library books selected by first graders. If tradebooks and other media can capitalize successfully on the six-year-old's need to escape, to live vicariously, to take risks, to gain revenge, to conquer the unconquerable, why not reading textbooks? *The Little Engine that Could*, and *Where the Wild Things Are*, are examples of different approaches in presenting this kind of content in tradebooks. The former book uses an inanimate object with human attributes, the latter book uses a human character with sometime-magical powers. In both stories, the impotent become omnipotent and the issue of gaining control over one's world is accomplished through fantasy material made relevant to the six-year-old. For the first grade child, there are realistic limits to where one can go and what one can do. Fantasy makes it possible to go and to do what is not possible under any other circumstances.

In conclusion, "content awareness" is basically what this book is all about and it is aimed at reaching all those people deeply concerned with reading instruction: Schools and departments of education, textbook authors and publishers, teachers, school administrators, reading specialists, curriculum and instructional consultants, librarians, and parents. The authors intended to create in them a "content awareness"— a sensitivity to the influence of textbook story content in teaching and motivating neophytes toward mastering the first R and toward socializing them to the attitudes valued by a democratic society. Both what is in the reading textbooks and what has been left out have been clearly described and discussed. The need for change has been documented. As is true in most situations, the easy part was to criticize. The more difficult next step was to locate and expose the weaknesses systematically, objectively and quantitively. Following this critical analysis, it was important to present suggestions and recommendations as to how to improve textbook story content. These steps have been accomplished and are covered in this volume. In addition, lists of tradebooks preferred by first graders in suburban and inner-city schools may be found in the Appendix. As an aid to selecting appropriate textbook stories, the readers of this book are referred to A Teacher's Guide for Selecting Stories of Interest to Children, (Zimet, Blom, & Waite, 1968). In this comprehensive cross-index, all of the 2,443 stories in both all-white and multiethnic primary reading textbooks are characterized by each of the dimensions discussed in Chapters 1, 5, and 7. This guide is aimed at facilitating the development of a program of differentiated primary reading instruction by those teachers, curriculum consultants and clinicians directly concerned with organizing and implementing such a program. For example, the users of this index would, in effect, be saying, "Given the characteristics of this child, I think he will be attracted by stories whose themes are Work Projects and whose characters are solely children." This represents an attempt, therefore, to match the story to the child. If concerned adults consicously pose this same problem about children needing to be motivated, they are more likely than not to be successful in selecting relevant story material.

Hopefully, the awareness and sensitivity to textbook story content fostered by reading this book will lead to the next crucial step—the development and implementation of action programs at various educational, business, and community levels—in higher education with programs involved in more effective teacher preparation, supervision, and curriculum development; in classrooms with teachers, curriculum consultants, and administrators concerned with the day-to-day instruction of children and where a responsive, success-oriented atmosphere prevails; with reading specialists confronted with the problems of remedial teaching where motivation plays such an important role; among school board members who determine budgetary issues and are frequently instrumental in textbook selection; with librarians who wish to see reading become a life-time loving habit; for parents who see success in reading as being an integral part of success and happiness in life; and, of course among writers and publishers of textbooks, where innovations and changes of any kind are going to have to prove profitable and are therefore dependent upon an informed, content-aware public.

REFERENCES

Zimet, S. G., Blom, G. E., & Waite, R. R. *A teacher's guide for selecting stories for children.—The content of first grade reading textbooks.* Detroit: Wayne State University Press, 1968.

APPENDIX A

RANK ORDER OF 71 BOOKS MOST FREQUENTLY CHECKED OUT OF A SCHOOL LIBRARY BY WHITE SUBURBAN FIRST GRADERS[1]

Title	Author	Frequency		
		Total	Boy	Girl
Hop on Pop	Dr. Seuss	22	8	14
Ten Apples Up on Top	T. Le Sieg	18	8	10
Golden Egg Book	M. Brown	17	6	11
Curious George Gets A Medal	H. A. Rey	16	13	3
Cecily G. and the 9 Monkeys	H. A. Rey	15	12	3
The Cat in the Hat	Dr. Seuss	14	6	8
Curious George	H. A. Rey	13	11	2
Where the Wild Things Are	M. Sendak	13	8	5
Please Don't Feed Horace	M. Young	12	5	7
Go, Dog, Go	P. D. Eastman	12	6	6
Millions of Cats	W. Gag	12	5	7
Curious George Rides A Bike	H. A. Rey	12	9	3
Nothing At All	W. Gag	11	7	4
Horton Hears A Who	Dr. Seuss	11	9	2
Katy and the Big Snow	V. Burton	11	7	4
Green Eggs and Ham	Dr. Seuss	11	7	4
Oliver	S. Hoff	11	3	8
Robert the Rose Horse	J. Heilbroner	11	6	5
How the Grinch Stole Christmas	Dr. Seuss	11	10	1
The Tale of Peter Rabbit	B. Potter	11	3	8
Red Light, Green Light	M. Brown	11	5	6
Horton Hatches the Egg	Dr. Seuss	11	6	5

Title	Author	Frequency		
		Total	Boy	Girl
On Beyond Zebra	Dr. Seuss	10	7	3
What Spot?	C. Bonsall	10	4	6
Huge Harold	B. Peet	10	4	6
The Fire Cat	E. Averill	10	4	6
Are You My Mother?	P. O. Eastman	10	4	6
Little Bear	E. Minarik	9	0	9
The 5 Chinese Brothers	C. H. Bishop	9	5	4
Little Black, A Pony	W. Farley	9	2	7
Two Little Bears	Ylla	9	5	4
I Was Kissed by a Seal at the Zoo	H. Palmer	9	3	6
Buttons at the Zoo	E. McCall	8	3	5
Cat and Dog	E. Minarik	8	1	7
Yertle the Turtle	Dr. Seuss	8	6	2
Stanley	S. Hoff	8	4	4
One Fish, Two Fish, Red Fish, Blue Fish	Dr. Seuss	7	5	2
Follow the Sunset	H. & N. Schneider	7	1	6
Mother Goose	K. Greenaway	7	2	5
Sad Day, Glad Day	V. Thompson	7	0	7
Jenny's Birthday Book	E. Averill	7	2	5
Curious George Takes a Job	H. A. Rey	7	5	2
Danny and the Dinosaur	S. Hoff	7	4	3
Little Chief	S. Hoff	7	3	4
Grizzwold	S. Hoff	7	2	5

144

APPENDIX A (continued)

Title	Author	Total	Frequency	
			Boy	Girl
Poppy Seed Cakes	M. Clark	7	1	6
Georgie	R. Bright	7	5	2
Dinosaurs	H. Zim	7	6	1
The House at Pooh Corner	A. Milne	7	2	5
Case of the Hungry Stranger	C. Bonsall	7	1	6
Bonnie Bess, the Weathervane Horse	A. Tresselt	7	5	2
Bennett Cerf's Book of Riddles	B. Cerf	7	4	3
Look Out for Pirates	I. Vinton	7	5	2
Pinocchio	C. Collodi	6	5	1
Marshmallow	C. Newberry	6	1	5
The Story of Babar, the Little Elephant	J. De Brunhoff	6	2	4
Bucky Button	E. McCall	6	3	3
Christmas in the Stable	A. Lindgren	6	1	5
Buttons and the Pet Parade	E. McCall	6	2	4
Happy Birthday to You	Dr. Seuss	6	2	4
Tale of Benjamin Bunny	B. Potter	6	0	6
Story about Ping	M. Flack	6	3	3
Sad Mrs. Sam Sack	A. Brothers & M. Botel	6	0	6
Finder, Keepers	W. Lipkind	6	1	5
Snow	Eastman & McKie	6	3	3
Prince Bertram the Bad	Lobel	6	3	3

145

APPENDIX A *(continued)*

Title	Author	Frequency		
		Total	*Boy*	*Girl*
Dr. Seuss's ABC	Dr. Seuss	6	1	5
Curious George Flies a Kite	H. A. Rey	6	5	1
Thidwick, the Big-Hearted Moose	Dr. Seuss	6	5	1
I Like Cats	E. W. & M. P. Dolch	6	0	6
The Outside Cat	J. Thayer	6	0	6

Source: Wiberg, J. L., and Trost, M. "Comparison of Content of First Grade Primers and Free Choice Library Selections," *Elementary English*, 48: 792-798, 1970. Copyright © 1970 by the National Council of Teachers of English. Reprinted by permission of the publisher and J. Lawrence Wiberg and Marion Trost. The original article appears in this book as Chapter 3.

APPENDIX B

RANK ORDER OF 39 BOOKS MOST FREQUENTLY CHECKED OUT OF A SCHOOL LIBRARY
BY BLACK URBAN FIRST GRADERS

			Frequency	
Title	Author	Total	Boy	Girl
Harry the Dirty Dog	G. Zion	8	5	3
Curious George Goes to the Hospital	H. A. Rey	8	3	5
Curious George Takes a Job	H. A. Rey	8	3	5
Lion	P. Du Bois	7	3	4
Boats on the River	M. Flack	7	3	4
How the Grinch Stole Christmas	Dr. Seuss	7	4	3
Cowboy Small	L. Lenski	7	5	2
Where the Wild Things Are	M. Sendak	7	4	3
Grandfather and I	H. E. Buckley	6	3	3
Bantie and her Chicks	J. Boreman	5	2	3
How, Hippo	M. Brown	5	3	2
And to think I Saw It on Mulberry Street	Dr. Seuss	5	2	3
Grizzwold	S. Hoff	5	2	3
Gone is my Goose	D. Koch	5	1	4
Randy's Dandy Lions	B. Peet	5	3	2
Wedding Procession of the Ragdoll and the Broom Handle and Who was in it	C. Sandberg	5	2	3
Quiet on Account of Dinosaur	J. Thayer	5	4	1

147

Title	Author	Total	Frequency	
			Boy	Girl
Whistle for Willie	E. J. Keats	5	0	5
Smallest Boy in Class	J. Beim	4	1	3
Witch of Hissing Hill	M. Calhoun	4	1	3
Drummer Hoff	B. Emberley	4	1	3
Be Nice to Spiders	M. B. Graham	4	3	1
Mr. Bumba Rides a Bicycle	P. A. Harwood	4	3	1
Bedtime for Frances	R. Hoban	4	3	1
Trouble with Spider	R. Kraus	4	2	2
Homework Caper	J. Lexau	4	4	0
Inch by Inch	L. Lionni	4	2	2
Chago	W. & M. Lipkind	4	2	2
Make way for Ducklings	R. McCloskey	4	2	2
Bad Bear	R. Neumann	4	3	1
Shapes	M. Schlein	4	1	3
Cowboy Tommy	S. Tousey	4	2	2
Circus in the Jungle	D. & A. Trez	4	2	2
Don't Be Scared Book	I. Vogel	4	3	1
Meanest Squirrel I Ever Met	G. Zion	4	1	3
Runaway Bunny	M. W. Brown	4	1	3
Wobble the Witch Cat	M. Calhoun	4	4	0
Take a Nap Harry	M. Chalmers	4	2	2
What Spot?	C. N. Bonsall	4	2	2

INDEX

149